Fiction!

Fiction!

Interviews with Northern California Novelists

by Dan Tooker and
Roger Hofheins

Photographs by
Dan Tooker

HARCOURT BRACE JOVANOVICH, INC./WILLIAM KAUFMANN, INC.

New York • *Los Altos*

ACKNOWLEDGMENTS

We wish to express our gratitude to the editors and publishers of the following magazines, where several of the interviews in this volume first appeared: *Pacific Sun, The Southern Review, Transatlantic Review,* and *Transfer.*

We wish to thank a number of people who helped us with various chores during different stages of this project. Vic Burnham, Martha Ford, Kathy Zetes and Phyllis Schaefer helped us transcribe tapes and type edited drafts. Mrs. Schaefer also helped us by taking down in shorthand Evan Connell's answers to our questions during our second meeting with him. Larry Sultan developed, contacted and printed the photographs in this book. David Koch of the Morris Library (Southern Illinois University) kindly let us use his bibliography of Kay Boyle's books published in the United States. He is completing a detailed bibliography on Miss Boyle and welcomes new entries. Finally, we wish to thank Nancy Rosenbloom for her editorial help in correcting the final manuscript.

Contents

TO THE WRITERS

"Devise, wit! write, pen!"

The idea for this book came from a series of interviews I was recording with painters and sculptors in the San Francisco Bay Area. One evening over dinner with Roger Hofheins, I suggested the idea of recording interviews with local novelists. Roger and I were both interested in fiction (Roger had completed his first novel and I was struggling with mine), and he liked the idea. By the end of the meal we had agreed to collaborate.

As almost no fiction is published in this part of the country, most novelists live here quietly, stepping into public view only when a new book is published. Kay Boyle, Wallace Stegner, and Herbert Gold are the most visible writers, and they formed the beginning of the list of people whom we wanted to interview. I heard James Leigh and Ernest Gaines read from their work at San Francisco State University and asked each of them for an interview. Leigh agreed immediately. Gaines was more skeptical. His book, THE AUTOBIOGRAPHY OF MISS JANE PITTMAN, had just been published and reporters were asking him for interviews. Having had some bad experiences, when I asked him for an interview he replied, "I'll do it if you read my work first."

We asked around and our list grew. Each writer we talked to suggested someone else, and we began reading that author's work. James Leigh told us about Evan Connell. Connell mentioned Alfred Coppel and Janet Lewis. Alfred Coppel and Peter Beagle told us about Jessamyn West. We soon had a list of more than fifty writers—all of them novelists—who live between Watsonville and Napa. Out of the fifty we chose twelve, selecting those authors whose work we liked best.

We didn't want to shape or direct the interviews as much as we wanted to get the writers to talk about, and thus reveal, themselves. Our questions were deliberately open-ended and often reflected our own concerns in writing. Some of our often-used questions were: "Why do you write?" "Is writing difficult?" "How do you begin a novel?" "How did you get started as a writer?" Other questions dealt with specific books or short stories, or the author's background. Don Carpenter's script writing suggested questions centered around the differences between writing for the screen or television, and writing novels and stories. We asked Leonard Gardner about his experiences working on the movie version of FAT CITY, and found similarities between his answers and Carpenters'. Because Jim Leigh was teaching and writing during the time of his interview, we asked him about the combination of those professions. Since he was our first subject in this series, and since we were both interested in the topic for our own information, we also asked him about the problems of publishing and the ways in which publishers work. We asked Janet Lewis about her approach to writing historical novels, and her use of source documents. We discovered that she believes faithfulness to historical fact is crucial; she creates the psychology and motivations of her characters to illuminate this historical reality.

While Roger and I enjoyed all of the interviews, much of the transcribing and editing was slow and tedious. Many of our transcripts were very long. Some came out to be as many as seventy pages, which we edited down to between ten and thirty pages, depending on how much interesting material we had. During the editing process we frequently combined answers. For example, we asked a writer a question and received a response. Later, in the middle of answering a different question, the writer would make reference to, and expand upon, the earlier response. In those instances we combined the answers under one question. Sometimes we found an interesting response standing alone, abandoned and out of place in the middle of a different answer. We didn't want to cut it out simply because it lacked a question, and so we "invented" an appropriate question to go with the answer. Although both of us were present during each interview, we decided to remain anonymous behind the italics.

From the transcripts we developed rough drafts, which we then sent to the authors. All of the writers made changes on the drafts. Most were minor changes, a few were major revisions. In the case of three writers, we found in reading their transcripts that we had missed important questions or had not picked up and followed through with some important answers; we went back to see them again.

We were pleased that the writers we had chosen turned out to be such a diverse group, their answers to our questions providing strong contrast to each other "What I like is that funny line between what's supposed to be real and what's supposed to be fantastic," Peter Beagle told us. In one of his novels, A FINE AND PRIVATE PLACE, his characters "live" in a cemetery. In one of his stories, a young man discovers that his girlfriend is a werewolf. Wallace Stegner is a realist, often weaving fact and fiction together in long novels with historical backgrounds. He believes in the "life chronological, rather than the life existential." James Leigh is a comic writer with a varying sense of humor. His DOWNSTAIRS AT RAMSEY'S is often hilariously funny. THE RASMUSSEN DISASTERS is closer to black humor, and NO MAN'S LAND is both funny and compassionate. Alfred Coppel writes novels of different genres, but he is best known for what William Hogan at the SAN FRANCISCO CHRONICLE termed "tension fiction," tightly woven action novels such as BETWEEN THE THUNDER AND THE SUN and THIRTY-FOUR EAST. Leonard Gardner and Don Carpenter write—quite differently— about people whose lives offer them little hope. Gardner's FAT CITY is a study in one man's self-delusion. GETTING OFF, one of my favorite Don Carpenter novels, is about a man coping with the breakup of his marriage. Kay Boyle's novels and stories, set in Europe and America, are autobiographical and romantic. The novels of Janet Lewis are based on historical fact. Ernest Gaines writes about black people's struggles in Louisiana. Evan Connell writes precisely about upper middle class lives. MRS. BRIDGE is a contemporary classic, and quite simply the best novel about the upper middle class in America that I have ever read. Herbert Gold is known for his fluid writing style which derives, in part, from his method of working. Jessamyn West's novels are about people who are, for the most part, essentially good. Her vision in both THE FRIENDLY PERSUASION and EXCEPT FOR ME AND THEE seem strikingly optimistic in their view of humanity.

I heard Ray West once mention that novelists usually write about the place where they spent their childhood because the earliest experiences are the deepest. This is certainly true of Ernest Gaines, who writes exclusively about Louisiana. Evan Connell's early books, THE PATRIOT, MRS. BRIDGE, several stories in THE ANATOMY LESSON AND OTHER STORIES, and then later in MR. BRIDGE, use his childhood home of Missouri. Leonard Gardner's FAT CITY is about Stockton, his home town; and four of Alfred Coppel's novels, A LITTLE TIME FOR LAUGHTER, THE LANDLOCKED MAN, HERO DRIVER, and NIGHT OF FIRE AND SNOW, use the peninsula region below San Francisco that he knows so well. Yet Jessamyn West's reasons for using Indiana as a backdrop for her fiction are different from those who draw upon the early part of their lives for the realism which personal experience can give. West prefers to invent characters, instead of writing about people she either knows or has known.

The literary influences on the writers proved as varied as the personal influences. Although the writers responded with the usual greats—Tolstoy, Turgenev, Chekhov, Faulkner, Hemingway, Dickens, Mann and Shakespeare—when asked who among the avant-couriers in their profession are especially important, influential, or useful to their own work, most of the writers mentioned an influence which revealed his personal concern. Don Carpenter spoke of B. Traven. Peter Beagle told us that he learned about style and economy from Robert Nathan. He also referred to Mikhail Bulgakov, Gabriel Garcia Marquez, T. H. White and George MacDonald Fraser. Herbert Gold mentioned Alberto Moravia and Raymond Queneau. Alfred Coppel refered to John O'Hara. Evan Connell spoke of A. E. Coppard and Thomas Mann.

All of the writers spoke freely about their working habits. Herbert Gold spoke of his writing as "semi-automatic" which he cleans up afterward. Ernest Gaines and Leonard Gardner admitted to being slow workers. Peter Beagle said, "If I've done two pages [a day] that's a lot." Evan Connell, Kay Boyle, and Alfred Coppel seem to spend the most time at the typewriter, and Wallace Stegner has been able to compartmentalize his time so that he could switch from teaching, to running the Stanford Writing Program, to writing, to lecturing and back to writing.

These writers agreed that each day's work is a discovery, remarking that they seldom adhere to whatever plan they might have had at the beginning of a book or story. Ernest Gaines told us:

> [Beginning] a novel is like getting on a train to Louisiana. All you know at the moment is that you're getting on the train, and you're going to Louisiana. But you don't know what the conductor is going to look like; you don't know who you're going to sit behind, or in front of, or beside; you don't know what the weather is going to be when you pass through certain areas of the country; you don't know what's going to happen South; you don't know all these things, but you know you're going to Louisiana. You know you're going by train, and that it's going to take so many hours, days . . .

Kay Boyle told us that she might begin a story sixty times over, tearing off the first page sixty times and throwing it across the room. Alfred Coppel said, "Beginnings are tough because you must capture your readers' attention and at the same time set the scene, introduce the characters, lay out the situation. That is why I might think about a novel for months before sitting down to write." Evan Connell said simply, "If you get the first sentence just right, you can go on."

It was clear from the interviews that most of the writers feel that revising is the most painstaking act in the writing process. "I'm not exaggerating," said Peter Beagle, speaking of THE LAST UNICORN, "when I say that there are images, paragraphs, and scenes in that book that I wrote forty times." Evan Connell, talking about his first novel, THE PATRIOT (published after MRS. BRIDGE), said that he wrote the entire book six times, and rewrote one chapter fourteen or fifteen times. Later, he told us, "I've never had a sentence turn up in the final form as it was in the beginning."

All of the writers admitted that ideas come in the process of writing. Jessamyn West spoke of her "compost heap," and Peter Beagle refered to his "swamp." The common term is "inspiration," unreliable thing that it is. When it doesn't come on command, Herbert Gold does a lot of exercising or walking, and Alfred Coppel either takes a drive in his car or goes fishing. Inspiration eventually returns and they then go on.

Reading over these interviews, which were made between 1972 and 1975, reveals universal joys and agonies of writing which should show anyone who has ever tried to write, or is simply curious about writers, that it is just as difficult for the experienced writer as the inexperienced. Alfred Coppel said: "Talent is cheap. But writing takes talent *plus* devotion, dedication—call it whatever you will. Discipline." "For myself," said Jim Leigh, "I've come to believe in the compulsion to write as a necessity, because what else is going to keep you going when there are so many alternatives? It's extremely hard to make a living and to write on the side. There's so much you have to give up, and why should you?"

It's the determination to write that creates books, and that is what these writers share. As Leonard Gardner said, "When I was working on FAT CITY, I had a motto over my desk, and that was: THE ART OF THE NOVEL IS GETTING THE WHOLE THING WRITTEN. That's the most difficult thing."

Dan Tooker
San Francisco, California
April, 1976

Fiction!

Peter S. Beagle

Although Peter Beagle has published two novels and a non-fiction book that are now widely circulated in paperback, he has made his living by writing Hollywood and television film-scripts and articles for HOLIDAY magazine and other periodicals. He prefers this to teaching and takes a certain pride in doing "a craftsman-like job" on his less serious writing. "I never expected to make a living from fiction," he told us. "I've been lucky."

He lives on a farm, which he owns, outside of Watsonville, with his wife Enid, their three children and a large assortment of animals, including a black cat named Gully Jimson, a goat, and Charles, a small poodle.

Below the house is a long barn, mostly empty. At the end of it there is an enclosed room which is Peter's office. Inside, there is a desk with a Hermes portable typewriter on top of it, an electric heater, several folding chairs, and shelves on the walls strewn with papers, scripts, and books. In a corner of the room a large cardboard box is filled with crumpled balls of typewriter paper. "Rejects," he told us. Through a window in front of his desk, Peter can look out on his farm while he is working. He likes the country and sometimes worries that the sprawl is reaching his farm. "Each year they get closer," he said.

We set up the tape recorder and Peter sat at his desk as we talked. He speaks quickly, like a New Yorker, but in his tone there is the same gentle irony that can be found in A FINE AND PRIVATE PLACE, THE LAST UNICORN, and I CAN SEE BY MY OUTFIT.

DT

Is it true you published your first book when you were very young?

Beagle: Yes. I've had an agent since I was seventeen. I published my first book when I was twenty-one. That was all I wanted. That was it. I didn't want anything else in the world. I was willing to give up everything if I could do just that. If you want something that badly, you get it. I was twenty-one and dumb about everything except writing.

That was A FINE AND PRIVATE PLACE?

Beagle: Yes.

When did you start writing?

Beagle: I started when I was seven, literally. My parents were remarkable. They never told me that writing was not a fit profession for a young man. I can remember writing stories in class. I wanted to imitate sounds. I love sounds. I was always excited by the sensuality of words and I wanted to copy that. I would imitate other writers. I haven't altogether lost that. THE LAST UNICORN starts off imitating half a dozen people: James Stephens, Thurber, T. H. White. And Lord Dunsany is always somewhere in the background.

Did you have any favorite fairy tales as a child?

Beagle: I loved the Greek ones, of course, and Irish ones for some reason. My grandfather wrote fairy tales in Hebrew. He wrote a book of fairy tales that was dedicated to me. I was ten months old when he died. His hope was that I would grow up to be a good Jew and read Hebrew. I didn't, but my mother used to read his things to me and translate as she went along. Also, my father was a natural storyteller. He would tell stories to me and the other kids in the neighborhood. I just grew up with that tradition and the idea that fairy tales were all right, that fantasy was all right. Nobody said they weren't. This is why when I write fantasy, I write as though it were the most natural thing in the world. I can't understand why people think it took daring to write a book about a unicorn. For me, it's daring to set a novel in California, like my new one; and even though it's a peculiar sort of fantasy, I set it in as real a town as I can imagine and pay attention to daily things like the clothes people wear and the way they decorate their homes. That's harder because I miss a lot of those things. I really don't notice stuff.

What causes you to begin a book, say A FINE AND PRIVATE PLACE?

Beagle: Usually there's just one idea. A FINE AND PRIVATE PLACE began because I happened to live next to Woodlawn cemetary and walked in it and played in it. It was one of the few green places in our part of the Bronx. I was walking along looking at the mausoleums and thinking, "Wow, you could live in one of these!" Essentially, that was the springboard. I know I was in some weird state of grace writing it. I got away with murder and made mistakes I would never make today.

For example?

Beagle: There's too much talk. I would have trimmed out a lot of the talk now. Also, there are images and turns of phrase I was so proud of that I would just edit out now. In those days I wanted to get everything in there. I find it less necessary to say everything now.

In the book people's spirits remain alive after physical death. The characters remain conscious so long as they continue caring about life. Eventually they stop caring and just fade away. Where did this idea come from?

Beagle: I made it up. I make things up as I'm writing. There's a very odd relationship between me and a piece of paper. Very commonly I'll start a chapter without knowing what's in it. Things come to flower that I have no idea I'm thinking about. The pattern I keep turning back to is that I seem to write books to find out what it is I'm writing about. In each case, with every book I've done, I've been wrong about what I thought it was. About two-thirds of the way through, I find out what book I'm supposed to be doing and then I go back and make it look easy. My new book is taking me four years to find out what it's about and who's in it. It would be better I suppose if I could think these things out first and plan. Al Young and I were saying almost simultaneously on the phone the other day, "Next one I outline!"

Are there people who actually do that?

Beagle: Poul Anderson, the science fiction writer, once told me he knows everything in advance, that the actual writing is the shortest part of the process. Sometimes, I think he does better than that might suggest. He's done a couple of books I really like. He almost *has* to outline to make a living writing science fiction. He has to be extremely prolific and has to know what he's doing. He can't afford to discover at the typewriter, as I do. I think Anderson and other people often have a lot of things knocking around in different stages of completion. I seem to do one thing at a time. It's a matter of energy. I'm slow and lazy about a lot of things. I really have to be forced into thinking more than superficially. If I don't have to think about a new character or situation, I won't. But if I get to a point where I've painted myself into six corners at once, I have to think, and something happens—some kind of concentration, dementia, or whatever—that I can't get unless there's that kind of insane pressure. Jim Houston says that writing novels is like juggling: you throw up one ball, then another, and another. The first one comes down, and then you're writing a novel.

THE LAST UNICORN *is perhaps your best known novel. How did that begin?*

Beagle: That's harder to tell. An image. I have a painting up in the house. A Spanish painter who married my cousin gave it to me when I was seventeen. It's a painting of unicorns fighting bulls. I've had that painting half my life and stared at it a lot. That's one of the things. Also, when I was six I read a book about a little girl who brings home a wild colt that turns out to be a unicorn. I've never forgotten it.

The book is filled with folklore. Did you do any research?

Beagle: Some. It's funny. I know more about unicorns now than I did then. I have Odell Shepard's THE LORE OF THE UNICORN which is the great work on unicorns. It compiles everything anybody's ever written or said about unicorns. But I didn't have it then. The novel might be different to some extent if I had. When I started the book, I was living with a friend in Cheshire, Massachusetts. I went to the library in Pittsfield to look things up. I discovered the Chinese had a unicorn. And in one funny encyclopedia there was just a line: "Doctor Olfert Dapper saw a wild unicorn in the Maine woods in 1673." It didn't say that he claimed to, but that he actually saw one. That's the reason for the dedication in the book. And that was about all I found. It wasn't much help.

So most of the book was pure invention?

Beagle: Yes. The quotes from Pliny that a hunter gives in the first chapter I found in the Pittsfield library, but the rest I made up. When in doubt—I'm discovering more and more—make something up. When I got into magazine writing, I got so involved in learning my trade and getting facts and dialog absolutely correct that I got out of the habit of making things up. I made up a character cold for my new book. His being is so subsumed into the personality of a medieval Scots Laird that he talks in a terrible Frank Yerbyesque

Scots burr. My editor at Viking wrote back saying, "I didn't know you knew so-and-so who's my best friend and talks like that." I'm discovering more and more you can't make things up. I made up a fifteen-year-old witch, and lately I think I've been meeting them.

You mentioned your non-fiction. How much of I SEE BY MY OUTFIT *is factual?*

Beagle: It's all factual. The dialog is as near as I remember it. The events are accurate. I thought it was a travel book. It's not. It's about having known someone for twenty years, since I was three years old, and coming to a point in my life where a lady and a family are ahead, and behind is all my childhood.

Are your fiction and non-fiction somehow related?

Beagle: Yes. In OUTFIT, Phil and I had our own particular world which involved a great deal of fantasy. We'd play games being other people and making things up. UNICORN is obviously a fairy tale, but there are games and jokes, as with Captain Cully and his band, that come largely from the games friends and I used to play. Much of the fantasy comes from very real games and imaginings. It's just extrapolated a little bit further.

In addition to the novels and the non-fiction, you've also done some short stories. We were wondering if something like "Farrell and Lila the Werewolf"* was part of a longer work?

Beagle: Farrell is the hero of the new novel. "Farrell and Lila the Werewolf" was the second story I wrote about Farrell. I don't write many short stories. That's the one I like more than anything I've published. The story just came: I thought, "Wouldn't it be funny if you were living with a girl, and she turned out to be a werewolf?" I think I was taking out the garbage at the time. I don't know where Farrell came from. It was a long time before I knew his first name was Joe. I wrote the story to see how it would come out.

Would you tell us something about the new book?

*Published by Capra Press as LILA THE WEREWOLF.

Beagle: It's called THE KNIGHT OF GHOSTS AND SHADOWS. The Berkeley Society for Creative Anachronism held a medieval tilt on the lawn of the Claremont Hotel which, God knows, looks enough like a castle. I thought, "What if the line blurred and things got out of hand and all this became real?" I could visualize them defending the hotel against a peasant insurrection by pouring boiling oil over the parapets.

Do you struggle for your plot, characters, and imagery or do they just come?

Beagle: Both. The things I struggle for usually don't come out very well, and I cut them. I think eighty-five percent of what I do is craft. I've been doing this a long time. I spend eight hours a day down here. You learn things. But fifteen percent, or ten percent, or whatever, is what I call the swamp. I don't understand the swamp, but I believe it's there. There's a point where I will have come as far as I can by craft. I'll walk around this office and tell the swamp aloud sometimes, "All right, I'd appreciate it if you'd gurgle something up, because I can't do any more by myself." I've come to believe that in a day, or two days, or when it damn well feels like it, the swamp will burp up a character I've never met or something that's never happened to me, because it's done it before. In that sense all those strange images and metaphors come out of the swamp.

How much do you get done in an eight hour day?

Beagle: If I've done two pages that's a lot. I put down a sentence and look at it for a while and push it around some and then add another sentence to it and see how that looks. I work a sentence at a time and then look at the paragraph. Jim Houston is the only person who ever picked up on my paying a lot of attention to the last lines of my paragraphs. I seem to think in terms of paragraphs, and they're like building blocks. After a while, there's a point where I finally know what I'm doing and then I don't think in terms of paragraphs, but just write. So much of it is instinct and learning to trust your instincts. I have a Hungarian friend who's a poet. He gave me a poem which goes, "Being a poet is an act of faith and great memory, like digging a ditch." And that is really all I do. It is faith, pure faith.

How do you revise?

Beagle: I do it as I go along, but still have to revise again at the end of the book. Sometimes at night I come half awake realizing, "Oh shit, I knew that was a lousy adjective. I can't stand it. Damn. I should go down to the barn and change it right now. It's a lousy adjective. I should have done better. Dummy!"

Does the revising take as long as the writing?

Beagle: No. It's usually fairly quick. When I'm finished with the draft, I'll go back through it. It will be at least fifty pages too long, and I'll take fifty pages out a sentence at a time. That's slow and hard, but I don't mind doing it.

What about plot considerations and making everything fit together? Do you do this as you go along?

Beagle: Yes, because if it bothers me I can't go past it. An exception is the scene in THE LAST UNICORN, the scene with Haggard and Lady Amalthea on top of the tower. That's the last thing I wrote. I usually write straight through and when I come to the end I stop. But that thing hung me up desperately. I knew it was important to the plot, but I didn't know what to do with it. Enid, my wife, finally got me to skip it and go on and do the rest of the book, which I hate to do. I think very linearly, very consecutively. Of all the scenes in that book, that one was written over and over. I'm not exaggerating when I say there are images, paragraphs, and scenes in that book that I wrote forty times. Sometimes I quit because I can't make them any better. At other times, on the fortieth try everything locks into place.

Have you ever been tempted to try a "realistic" novel?

Beagle: My second novel was realistic. It was awful and unpublished, but even it kept sliding off into fantasy. It's the way I think. What I like is that funny line between what's supposed to be real and what's supposed to be fantastic, the line where suddenly you aren't sure where you are. One of my heroes is Gabriel Garcia Marquez, the Columbian writer. He does it all the time. He can be writing a perfectly serious novel about the exploitation of the resources and the crops and the peasants of South America by outsiders and it explodes into a fantastic, improbable scene. It will rain for forty-two years and then not rain for another eight, both of which he treats perfectly casually. Now, it doesn't rain for forty-two years in that part of the world, but near enough. Bruce Jay Friedman said in an introduction to a book of black humor: "Just now, as I write this, the wisest minds in Christendom are sitting down trying to decide if it's all right to forgive the Jews for killing Christ. How can I make up anything crazier than that or more fantastic? I'm just tagging along doing the best I can."

You and Robert Nathan are close friends. Has he been an influence?

Beagle: I read him when I was in high school and college. I learned a good deal from him about style and economy. In 1964 a mutual friend, John Weaver, introduced us. We've been corresponding ever since. I visit him in Los Angeles whenever I can. There aren't many heroes or villains in Nathan's books. There are people, blundering along, tripping over each other, and trying to stay warm. He can do a thing I still can't do: he's absolutely at home in time. Nathan can make the supposedly plausible and implausible flow in and out of each other, and that's something I want to do. Look, he wrote a novel at the age of seventy-eight in which a man meets a girl at Stonehenge who may be a modern hippy or who may just be Merlin's enchantress Nimue.

How do you feel about Tolkien?

Beagle: Tolkien obviously means something. I felt THE LAST UNICORN was completely free of his influence, and then I realized much later that, of course, he's there. He's not the greatest of the fantasy writers. It's just his fantastic imagination that created that world from the inside out. It's not the style, not even the story that Tolkien leaves behind him, it's that enormous world. T. H. White is a much better writer and means much more to me.

Are there any other writers you'd like to mention?

Beagle: Jim Houston and Al Young. We've known each other a long time. We rub off on each other. I'll do a sentence sometimes and think that I wouldn't have written it like that if I hadn't known Al for twelve years. Or I wouldn't have done that crowd scene if I hadn't watched Jim Houston doing things with crowd scenes. Jessamyn West is great. I'm delighted with George MacDonald Fraser. His Flashman novels—the nineteenth century seen through Flashman's eyes—are just superb. I think Nabokov is a genius although he makes me mad enough to throw the book across the room. He's a mean old bastard.

His attitude toward his characters?

Beagle: Toward his characters. Toward people. Things that come out. But he's a beauty. I don't know anybody who works with language the way he does. I can't read him while I'm working because I try to do that. And his attitude toward time, I'm fascinated with that. Then there's Bulgakov who wrote THE MASTER AND MARGARITA. You read that and it's like a dead man shaking hands with you. You suddenly feel, "That man is working my side of the fence."

In THE CALIFORNIA FEELING you express an extreme dislike for Walt Disney. . . .

Beagle: I grew up on Disney like everybody else. I absorbed a lot of Disney attitudes, and then when I got older I began to notice that Disney was a machine, turning out a certain product that reduced everything to Disney formulas. Finally, he nailed me with two of my favorite books in the whole world. I was so angry and appalled at what he, or it, or whatever, had done to THE SWORD IN THE STONE and THE JUNGLE BOOK that I made a promise to myself that I would never let Disney do anything of mine. So, when the whole question of Disney animating THE LAST UNICORN came up, I turned it down flat. If I ever meet T. H. White in the afterlife, I never want to have to explain why I went to Disney after what he did to THE SWORD IN THE STONE.

Can you put your finger on what Disney does?

Beagle: What can I tell you? He takes the balls out and replaces them with the cute little bareass of an angel. With Disney the tendency is always to do something cute. The public has been educated to accept what he turns out. There could have been a good movie of THE JUNGLE BOOK. The Disney people simply knew there didn't have to be.

There are some people who don't take fantasy very seriously. How do you react to that?

Beagle: I had a fairly worked-out argument, but enough. I'm thirty-four now and I've been doing this for a long time. I just do it because I like it. But, look, I've been lucky. When I started, I was writing a fantasy novel that could easily have been tossed into a bag with forty or fifty others and given to whoever it was who used to review science fiction for THE NEW YORK TIMES. Instead, I've always been treated as a serious writer. What the line is, I'm not sure. I know good science fiction writers who could certainly stand to be treated like real people. But the line is breaking down. Books by J. G. Ballard and Heinlein get reviewed now in the front pages of the Sunday TIMES. Nobody's quite sure where the line is now. They knew when I was in college. Poetry was T. S. Eliot, novels were Hemingway and a few others. That's all changing.

Why do you think?

Beagle: Many people, especially younger people, are coming to believe that there may be more than one reality. I remember a great line delivered by my younger brother who is a trained historian and a Marxist and an activist. He said, "I'm slowly coming grudgingly to believe that there are some things in the universe that Dialectical Materialism doesn't cover." I think people are less willing to accept flat definitions of what is real and what is not. There's that. The other thing, of course, is just plain desperation. You can hear it in the music. Suddenly there is a desperate swing back to the old styles of music. I know where it comes from. It comes from a hunger for that sort of time, walking down the street singing that sort of tune. Now you have all the UFOs suddenly being seen. This time you can really smell the hunger. There's a desperation for somebody to come down and get us out of this.

Before we go, could you tell us what you think it takes to write good fantasy, what the requirements are?

Beagle: There's at least one requirement, and I suppose the others share it: Jesus, you have to believe it. Recently a publisher sent me a book that's coming out. It's a fantasy by a writer of realistic novels. It's a big deal that this writer takes time off to write a fantasy. Writing fantasy just ain't that easy. They wanted me to write a blurb for the jacket, but the book's dreadful. Take a master like E. B. White. He believes what he's doing. There's no condescension in the man's work. It's the detail among other things. White takes it seriously. When he has Stuart Little lowered down the drain or driving a small car, he gives a lot of attention to what that drain was like to a small boy-mouse or mouse-boy. He takes nothing for granted with that happy little pastel brush of cuteness. Stuart's boat is a *real* boat, and he's on it. There's no marshmallow smudging at the edges. White's Stuart has dignity. It's very hard to do that. I remember Stuart meeting the telephone linesman and commenting that it is a nice day. And the linesman says, "Yes, it is. I'm looking forward to climbing my poles." No one ever said that I suppose, but they ought to. Are you looking forward to climbing your poles? Very few people are, whatever their poles happen to be.

NOVELS

A Fine and Private Place. New York: The Viking Press, 1960. (Delta, 1963; Ballantine Books, 1969.)

The Last Unicorn. New York: The Viking Press, 1968. (Ballantine Books, 1969.)

SHORT STORIES

***Lila the Werewolf.** Capra Press Chapbook, 1974.

*Published only in paperback.

NON-FICTION

I See By My Outfit. New York: The Viking Press, 1965. (Ballantine Books, 1966, 1971.)

The California Feeling. New York: Doubleday & Company, 1969. (Doubleday, 1971.)

American Denim. New York: Harry N. Abrams, 1975.

The Lady and Her Tiger. New York: E. P. Dutton, 1976. [With Pat Derby.]

Kay Boyle

Kay Boyle has lived and worked in San Francisco since 1963, when she accepted a teaching position in the creative writing department at San Francisco State University. She owns a large Italianate Victorian house in the Haight-Ashbury district which she shares with four students. Kay lives on the third floor where it is quiet and sunny. Downstairs, a full bookcase covers one wall of the formal dining room. Several shelves are filled with many of the thirty-six books she has written. Her social concerns are evident on the front door of the house where a poster proclaims: "Bring the monster down. End the air war." And on the door into the living room another poster written in English, French, and Arabic: "Open the Shah's jails. Free all political prisoners."

With teaching commitments and her involvement in social causes Kay is pressed for time to write. When she is not teaching or correcting student's stories, she spends twelve to fourteen hours a day at the typewriter, which she rests on her knees as she writes in bed.

The interview took place in the downstairs living room during the time she was in the final writing stages of her recent novel, THE UNDERGROUND WOMAN. She seems to possess enormous energy. She is elegant, and aristocratic in manner, laughs easily, and seemed to enjoy being interviewed. On writing, she told us: "Sometimes things don't turn out as well as you'd hoped, but as Sherwood Anderson once said, 'There's always more paper and more ink. The next one will be better.' "

DT

Why did you want to be a writer?

Boyle: I didn't want to be a writer. I just was one. I always wrote, ever since I was very, very young. And before I could write, I would tell my poems and stories to my mother.

Did you begin writing poetry or fiction?

Boyle: As a child, both. And paintings, too, of course. Then my sister and I, when we were twelve or thirteen, started a magazine which my grandfather paid for, and we wrote serials and all sorts of things. We just never thought of doing anything but writing, or painting, or music. My sister studied piano, and I studied violin. We never dreamed of buying Christmas presents for the family, for instance. We made books for the birthdays and other occasions. One book had a poem in it called "Arise, Ye Women," which I'd love to have now to give to women's lib people to show that I do care about women's independence although I'm not actually into the movement. My feeling about the women's liberation movement is that it is essentially a conservative movement, as, of course, the

Black Panther Party was as well. I would like to see something more revolutionary taking place.

Were you encouraged very strongly by your mother?

Boyle: Yes, completely. I would never have done anything if it hadn't been for her.

What was your father's reaction to all of this?

Boyle: Well, my father was one of those very silent and introverted people who suffered very much. My sister and I never had much contact with him because he was a frustrated person who couldn't communicate his feelings. He probably resented my mother very much, which we didn't realize then—resented her ideas, which were extraordinary. God knows where they came from. She didn't know any writers or painters well, with the exception of Charles Sheeler, Lewis Browne, and the photographer, Alfred Steiglitz. She would read Gertrude Stein aloud to us, and we were familiar with the sculpture of Brancusi and the paintings of Marcel Duchamp at a very early age. One of my childhood memories is of being taken to the Armory Show in 1913, where Marcel Duchamp's "*Nude Descending a Staircase*" had to be surrounded by police because the crowd wanted to throw eggs and tomatoes at it, or even to slash the canvas. Mother accepted me and my work as she accepted James Joyce, or Gertrude Stein, or Brancusi, or any serious artist. Because of her, I knew that anyone who wrote, or anyone who painted, or anyone who composed music, had a special place in life. And so, when I got to Paris, and really met these people who were accomplishing things, I felt I belonged with them, because Mother brought me up in that quite simple feeling.

In your autobiography, you described yourself as painfully shy.

Boyle: I was. I'm making up now for all the years I didn't talk. The first years I started teaching, I couldn't talk at all. I was miserable; but now I talk and make others miserable.

Do poetry and fiction come from the same well?

Boyle: Yes, definitely.

So, you've never felt a poet can't write fiction, or a fiction writer can't write poetry?

Boyle: No, not for a moment. Take Borges. Borges' short stories are better known to students and the public than his poetry. But he says quite simply that those who haven't read his poetry don't understand him at all.

What happens in the process of turning experience into fiction?

Boyle: Within one?

Yes.

Boyle: One gets very depressed. One can't make it come out right. One is in agony the whole time. One finds every excuse one possibly can not to sit down and write that piece of fiction as one feels one must write it. You see, I didn't have much of a formal education. I don't think I would have written all the books I did, over thirty books, had I realized that other people had already written everything there was to be said. I thought I had to tell people these things, because they hadn't been said before. That's why I felt compelled to write.

How much of your work is based on personal experience?

Boyle: All of it. It's twisted around, made into one thing or another, but it's all personal experience.

Autobiographical?

Boyle: In a sense. Fictionalized.

Where does fact end and fiction begin?

Boyle: In the novels?

Yes.

Boyle: I have no idea. Sometimes the girl that I started out with, who had my experiences, turns out to be a very different person than I was. One doesn't know what's going to happen.

Do the characters take over?

Boyle: Yes. And that's when I think you're doing well, when the characters come to life. They take the story somewhere else from where you had planned.

And they take the story out of your personal experience?

Boyle: It has happened to an extent. I've lived in so many countries and seen so many people, I can draw on a good deal without having to imagine too much. But, of course, I have imagined some episodes in the books.

Is there a central thing that has motivated all of your writing?

Boyle: Well, I think social or political comment or humanitarian comment has, in one way or another It started out in the early stories writing about black people. I remember we had black servants, and I felt very strongly about this.

I understand that in the Thirties your books were sometimes given bad reviews because they were not considered social commentary. Is this true?

Boyle: Well, it may be, but it's not very interesting. I believe at that time . . . I was living in Europe . . . and I believe in America at that time many of the reviewers were communist party members and I think they approached all work from that point of view. I think if a book is alive and well-written and expresses the author's viewpoint, that's all you have to care about. THE NEW MASSES, I remember, gave me a bad review because I had a nobleman as a heroic figure in one or two stories. In other words, I was not following the party line. There's also the fact that many people couldn't "identify" with the characters in my novels, and that's always a drawback to popularity. And although three of my books have been translated into French, they didn't have a wide circulation in France, and the reason for that is very clear to me. In a foreign country, they aren't particularly interested in reading what an American thinks about their country. They prefer regional American writers, and I think they're right.

Do your political feelings influence your writing?

Boyle: I think that would be inevitable. You see, the thing that makes me want to write is that I want to communicate things I believe, or speak of injustices that are being done, or of some deep emotional experience. But what really makes me excited about writing are the characters. A character may be active in some political or social way, like the man in "The White Horses of Vienna," the doctor. He was a fascinating man. That story won the O'Henry Award for the best story of the year, with Clifton Fadiman dissenting. He said it was a pro-Nazi story, which it wasn't at all. I was trying to show in that story—I think most people understood—that even very fine, very courageous people in desperate moments in their nation's life can be taken in by certain kinds of propaganda. Hitler was pouring propaganda into Austria about great economic changes once the Anschluss with Germany would take place. He promised employment to an almost totally unemployed country, and that people would have enough to eat again. And this doctor who had suffered very much, had been a prisoner of war in Russia, was, in his hope for a new society and a new world, taken in by it all.

You have written poetry, short stories, novels, non-fiction and memoirs. Which do you think has been the most successful?

Boyle: Short stories. I think it's because I've been able in my short stories to be less subjective, not to have that figure of an American girl, or an American woman, as a central figure, as she is in my longer fiction. I got very tired of doing that in my novels, so I wrote GENERATION WITHOUT FAREWELL, in which I had a German newspaperman as the central character. It was difficult to do, but it was very good discipline, having to put myself entirely into another's state of mind and state of being. MONDAY NIGHT is another novel where I got away from that feminine American figure, and that's why I like it the best.

Why is it easier to get away from the American girl in short stories?

Boyle: Because you don't have to sustain that particular, objective figure for such a long time. It's easier to stay in another person's mind for briefer lengths of time, and thus the ordeal is less demanding.

Is there any difference besides length between writing a short story and a novel?

Boyle: Yes, I think there's a lot of difference. I think one of the basic differences is that the characters do have to develop in the novel. They have to get somewhere else. They have to change, either for better or worse. In a short story there doesn't have to be the same degree of development, because the characters and the situation can be dealt with as caught in a particular moment in time.

Do you think you have a particular facility for writing short stories?

Boyle: No. I don't have a particular facility for writing anything. Everything is terribly hard to write, and it gets worse every year; every book I write is harder than the last one.

What was the literary revolt of Paris all about?

Boyle: One of the things it was about was a departure from the fixed mold into which the English language had solidified. The American language was just beginning, started by, in part, Mark Twain, then Sherwood Anderson, and about the same time as Anderson, Gertrude Stein. Then Hemingway came in and profited by the barriers others had already broken down. Joyce's writing was also a revolt against the hardened mold of the English language, but his approach was essentially different, for he was an Irishman in rebellion against religion as well.

So you think the revolt was primarily semantic?

Boyle: It was called by Eugene Jolas and the sur-realists "The Revolution of the Word."

What about the revolt in terms of the formal structure of the novel?

Boyle: Well, there was no real revolt there, at that time, was there, except for ULYSSES? Joyce was much closer to the French writers, who were experimenting in the Twenties, than he was to the Americans or the English.

Do you think the revolt was successful?

Boyle: If you mean the "Revolution of the Word," yes, I think so. Perhaps we ourselves didn't succeed in what we set out to do with such fervor, but we certainly cleared the way for people to go ahead with what we had begun. Hemingway could never have been Hemingway without Sherwood Anderson and Gertrude Stein as forebears. He simply couldn't have done it. And it wouldn't have happened in such a sustained form, with such unity of purpose, without Eugene Jolas, who conceived of the revolution of the word. He also had been closer to German and French writers than to American writers. His magazine, TRANSITION, printed stories, poems, and essays in French and German as well as English.

Why was it based in Paris?

Boyle: People don't like to hear this, but one of the reasons why Paris was such a center for foreign artists and writers in the Twenties was that it was a very cheap place to live. You could live for a couple of dollars a week. And you could publish books and magazines there for very small sums. When the monetary exchange got bad, people moved out. We went to Austria and stayed there many years. Robert McAlmon went to Berlin. But for a decade or more, the exchange was fantastic for an American living in France. I lived and worked in Paris for two years, first in Raymond Duncan's commune, and then as secretary to a fashion writer. I had lived as the wife of a Frenchman in Normandy and Brittany and in the south of France. There were also three years in England. We lived abroad for twenty years, one reason being that we didn't have the money to come back.

Do you think Hemingway has had more influence than he deserves?

Boyle: Well, I don't know how much influence he's had. One doesn't read many stories written his way now. I've had only one student in the last eight years studying him as a major author. He doesn't seem to be popular on college or university campuses. I would say that Gertrude Stein is more respected now.

How do you explain Hemingway's decline in popularity? Do you think it's deserved?

Boyle: Yes. After the early stories in IN OUR TIME and his novel A FAREWELL TO ARMS, I don't think he had anything much to say. Nabokov said one time: "I read a novel of Hemingway's sometime in the 1940's. I can't remember the title, and I don't know whether it was about bells, bulls, or balls." I think that's an astute criticism of Hemingway.

What about Fitzgerald?

Boyle: Well, I just was never enchanted by his writing. I have reread THE GREAT GATSBY several times because some of my students were studying Fitzgerald. I cannot get the same thing out of it that everyone else seems to. The same is true of TENDER IS THE NIGHT.

Is it the class of people he was writing about?

Boyle: Possibly, but it was also his way of writing. He was certainly not doing anything new with the novel.

Do you think there's an obligation for a modern writer to continue experimentation?

Boyle: I don't think it's an obligation, but I think any good writer should want to experiment. There are some very fine writers who are satisfied with the old forms. Eudora Welty is one, and she is a tremendous writer. This is also true of Malamud. But I think that the most exciting writers are finding new ways of saying things. Mark Twain, Gertrude Stein, Faulkner are among those who did. John Hawkes is another in our time.

Getting back to the agony of writing, if it's torture, and if it's agony, why write?

Boyle: Take away that "if"! Because afterwards, when you really feel you've said something as you wanted to say it, it's a great satisfaction, a tremendous reward. Also, if you write something that you feel has reached people who haven't been reached in that way before, it's a very exciting thing to know.

Do you think that fiction has the power to change men's minds?

Boyle: Well, men probably have to do that for themselves, but it can have the power to reveal each person to himself. But then you have that quote from Thornton Wilder, who said, "The miser in the audience never recognizes himself as the miser on the stage." So sometimes the writer fails in revealing a person to himself.

You said any good writer should want to experiment with style. . . .

Boyle: Well, let's put it this way. Any good and imaginative writer wants to find new ways of saying things. This is important, so as to hold one's own interest as well as that of the reader. Sometimes as I'm writing, I stop short and think, "Oh, God, this is terribly boring. I must find a way of saying it more clearly and sharply than it's ever been said before."

Another thing: in the 1920's, Beckett wrote a beautiful essay about Joyce. It appeared in TRANSITION. He said Joyce is not writing *about* something, he is writing *something*. When he describes a candle, you feel the grease, or wax, or smell the burning wick, exactly as if you held the candle. Beckett is one who insists that you cannot possibly divide content from style. Take Dante's IN-FERNO, which influenced both Joyce and Beckett so profoundly. It was the inferno itself that Dante gave us, not a description that we could forget once we closed the book.

Is there a particular point of view, or way of telling a story, that you like best, or that you feel most comfortable with?

Boyle: I never feel comfortable with writing, let's face it. I haven't met many writers who do feel comfortable with writing. Sometimes I start a short story sixty times over, tear off the first page sixty times and throw it across the room.

What about writing in the first person?

Boyle: No. I must say I think the first person narrows the possibilities. I have written quite a number of stories in the first person, but I don't think it is the most satisfying way. The "I" is always a bit self-conscious, a bit embarrassing, even when printed small, as cummings practiced it.

Are there any other reasons why you object to the first person?

Boyle: In the first place, it has to be a very simple story if told in the first person, because that person has to be everywhere. That "I" has to be everywhere. Or else overhear things, or peek through keyholes. Then it's difficult for the first person to know all the complexities of the interactions between people. The device of having the "I" the confidante of a number of people is never very convincing.

Has your writing changed, or developed over the years?

Boyle: No. It's exactly the way it was when I was ten years old. It's quite true. My ideas are the same, my convictions are the same, although the spelling and syntax have slightly improved.

When you begin a novel or a story, do you have the whole thing in mind when you sit down to write, or just a character?

Boyle: Usually, just a few characters, and perhaps a situation that has troubled or excited me. But the end is sometimes very different from what I had anticipated.

Do you know whether it will be a novel or a story when you begin?

Boyle: Oh, yes. In a novel you find yourself creating more of a setting than you would in a short story.

How do you know before you sit down whether it's going to be a novel or a story?

Boyle: I know principally because of the amount of time I have. If I've got three or four months before me, I could be starting a novel. If I have only a few weeks, it's got to be a story.

Do any of your novels begin as stories?

Boyle: I don't think so. There were chapters of my novel YEAR BEFORE LAST that appeared in TRANSITION as stories. But I was feeling my way into the novel when I wrote them. At that time I had not written a published novel, although I had several drafts of novels done.

Have you written any plays?

Boyle: I wrote one play, but I've never been able to finish it. I think probably someone else will have to finish it for me someday. As far as I can make out, I haven't got a first act. I thought I had a first and second act, and lacked a third act, but, when I looked at it a few months ago, I realized I had a second and third act, and no first act. It's a play about Rosa Luxembourg in prison in Germany because of her political beliefs, and it's very relevant to our times. She is a woman I admire deeply.

Why can't you finish it?

Boyle: I started it about fifteen years ago, and periodically I take it out and look at it. It just isn't right.

Is it because you cannot use description in writing a play?

Boyle: Yes, I miss the opportunity to describe, but I suppose I could get over that. But I just can't see it on the stage somehow, this play. It doesn't look right. Perhaps someday I'll meet someone who will write the first act.

When you write, do you work from an outline?

Boyle: Never. I can't even give an outline to my publisher, which frequently disturbs him a great deal.

Do you ever feel like an adventurer, or do you feel a sense of doubt when you don't know where you're going next?

Boyle: I feel both of those things.

Is this exciting?

Boyle: No.

Horrifying?

Boyle: It's depressing. I'm in that state at the present time with the novel that I'm trying to finish. I haven't been able to look at it since last September, and I realize I'll probably have to take out the long chapter that I was just finishing, which was about twenty pages long. I think it has gone wrong somewhere.

How long have you been working on it?

Boyle: Oh, about two-and-a-half-years. It was supposed to have been handed in to my publisher a year ago January. I took off from teaching one semester last year to write it, and I wrote all last summer. And I still haven't got it done.

Is it set in San Francisco?

Boyle: Yes. It's set partly in the Santa Rita jail. It also goes into a description of a commune in Roxbury, Massachusetts. So it too is relevant to our times, and the publisher keeps saying, "You must get it done, because these things you are writing about are uppermost now in people's minds." But what can you do? You can't push a hundred or more students aside and do your own work.

Do you think about the changing market when you're writing?

Boyle: No. I don't think that ever comes into my head. That's probably one thing that is good, I mean, the fact that I've never had great financial success, except for my novel AVALANCHE. It was the first book about the French resistance, and it ran as a serial in THE SATURDAY EVENING POST, and sold two hundred and fifty thousand copies to the Armed Forces. I have met many men who were airmen during the war who said they had to read that book before parachuting into France, so they would understand the situation and the opposed positions of the French people. It's a novel, but very factual.

Do you ever get writer's block to the point where you give up on a piece of work? Do you have drawers filled with unfinished manuscripts?

Boyle: No. Only my play.

So you stick with a thing until you get it right?

Boyle: Yes, and I try to persuade my students to do just that, because I think you're utterly defeated if you say, "Well, I'm going to throw this story away and start something else."

Which was your most difficult book to write?

Boyle: They're all difficult.

Would you set a book aside and then come back to it after working on something else?

Boyle: I usually don't have enough time for that. Oh, yes, there's one more thing I've set aside, but it's going to be finished. A long time ago, when my husband and I needed money very, very badly, I contracted to write a *modern* history of Germany (not a history of modern Germany). Only fiction writers were asked to write in this series that was being edited by John Gunther. At the time I said to my husband, "I don't know a damned thing about history." But my husband was Austrian and had his Ph.D. in history, so he said, "Don't worry, we'll do it together. It will be all right." So I got quite a lot of it done, but not nearly enough, only about three hundred pages. Then, after my husband died, I got up to Bismarck, and then I woke up one morning last June, and said to myself, "I cannot write about Bismarck and the men around him. If I do, I'll lose my mind." So I talked to my publisher, a great man, Ken McCormick, and I said, "The only good chapters in that book are about women, German women. They were the first women to have a peace movement in the world. They were against every war their men foisted upon them. I want to turn this into a book about German women." And he said, "Fine." So, I'm scrapping a lot of that manuscript, and after I finish the novel this summer, I'm going to go back and complete the history. It's called THE NOBLEST WITNESSES. One of my favorite chapters in the book is about Charlemagne. Now I can twist the Charlemagne chapter around to include it in the book about women because he had a great many women in his life. And I can make the women and what he did to them important, and not Charlemagne himself. Had correspondence or diaries of Frau Bismarck or the wives of other German monsters been available, I might have been able to finish the history as it was first conceived.

You seem to be very disciplined. Do you set aside a certain time of day to write?

Boyle: I try to write every minute I can when I haven't got student papers to do, which is not the case now. I have forty papers to do before tomorrow morning.

Well, what is your routine in the summer, when you're not teaching?

Boyle: I get up, have breakfast, and start work. When I get tired, I take a nap or have lunch. Then I start work again, and I go until I'm too tired to go on. When I was younger I could work until one or two in the morning, but I can't do that anymore. I can't go much beyond eleven o'clock at night. Everything is an interruption to me, and I resent interruptions, so I have an unlisted telephone number, and I can't hear the doorbell at the top of the house where I live.

Do you revise as you go along?

Boyle: Oh, yes.

Do you have to get one chapter right before you can go on to the next one?

Boyle: Sometimes, not always.

So, when you're finished with the book, it's a finished piece of work?

Boyle: Never. I have a typist I give the chapters to when I'm done with them, when I consider them pretty much finished, and then by the time he brings them back, I've changed my mind. And I never read anything after it's published, because I know I'd want to change everything again.

Which writers have influenced you?

Boyle: I would probably have to say different people every year, but I know D. H. Lawrence had a great influence on me, and Dostoevsky. The ones that are supposed to have influenced me really have not. Chekhov did not. I love his work, but I don't write that way.

Why Lawrence and Dostoevsky?

Boyle: Because of their tremendous humanity. Lawrence had a great feeling about people. It comes out in some of his books more than others. In a book called THE BOY IN THE BUSH set in Australia, for example, the humanity is warmly and richly expressed. That is a fascinating book, but not one of his best known.

How would you respond to the women's liberation attitude about Lawrence as a male chauvinist?

Boyle: I don't agree with that at all. I think there are male chauvinists on the literary scene, and obviously Norman Mailer is one, but Lawrence was a true artist and a very complex man.

Why Dostoevsky? The same basic reason as Lawrence?

Boyle: Yes. Dostoevsky possessed a terriffic curiosity about people, much as Henry Miller has.

How do you feel about Katherine Mansfield and Anaïs Nin?

Boyle: Katherine Mansfield's stories came into prominence when I was in my early twenties, I guess. And people were always saying to me, "You should read Katherine Mansfield." I did. I rather liked her work, but I didn't like her overuse of the words "tiny" or "little." They set limits on her capacities. Then when I read her letters, I was really horrified. The smallness of her approach to life, cutting her off from so much, and the terrible guilt that burdened her about her brother's death. Anaïs Nin: what can I say? That isn't the kind of writing I respond to. I find it difficult to explain the popularity of Anaïs Nin when women writers of such substance as Grace Paley, Mary Lavin, May Dikeman, and Eudora Welty are writing.

Do you recommend teaching as a way for young writers to support themselves?

Boyle: No, but that's something the young writer has to find out for himself. You can't get a job anyway, now, so I don't think it's a question of any real importance. I have literally dozens of Ph.D. students who are trying to get jobs. And almost every taxi driver in New York City, strangely enough, has a Ph.D. in Physics. That was at one time supposed to be a way to assure you of a teaching job, but the scene has changed. I don't remember ever telling a young writer to try to support himself by writing, but I do remember Camus saying he always had a job as an actor, as a director, or in a publishing house, so that his writing would not have to suffer. He could write what he pleased, but he would make his money in other ways.

How about the future of the novel?

Boyle: Oh, dear.

Does it have a future?

Boyle: How can I possibly say? Certainly the novel in its old form is finished. It died several years ago in France. It doesn't exist in Germany either.

What's replacing it?

Boyle: The anti-novel. I suppose the anti-hero.

Robbe-Grillet?

Boyle: Yes. And Heinrich Böll in Germany.

Who among the younger writers do you most like?

Boyle: A student of mine named Shawn Wong and another student named Steven Gray.

In writing short stories for large circulation magazines, have you ever had to alter anything to fit editorial policy?

Boyle: Yes.

How did you go about doing this?

Boyle: For instance, in AVALANCHE, which ran in THE SATURDAY EVENING POST, as I said before, the editor told me I couldn't have the girl's parents both French. One of them would have to be American to make it acceptable to an American public. So I made—I forget—the mother, I think, American. Also, the hero had to come in every twenty pages because of the serial requirements. So I dragged him in every twenty pages, and I left it that way when it was published as a book.

Is that frustrating?

Boyle: No, I didn't alter the spirit of the story. I said what I meant in that book, romanticized as it was. But I remember once an editor of COLLIER's was going to get out a whole issue on, "If the Soviet Union Invades America," and on the cover they were going to have a picture of Stalin standing on the White House steps. I was to write an article from the point of view of mothers with children trying to live in Soviet-occupied America. I said, "What in the name of God are you talking about?" He said, "Look, we'll pay you five thousand dollars for the article." The idea was that writers of this country were to contribute their part to the Cold War. You can see how impossible it would be to go along with anything like that.

NOVELS

Plagued by the Nightingale. New York: Cape and Smith, 1931. Published in hardback by the Southern Illinois University Press, Carbondale, Ill., 1966.

Year Before Last. New York: Harrison Smith, 1932. Published in hardback by the Southern Illinois University Press, Carbondale, Ill., 1969.

Gentlemen, I Address You Privately. New York: Smith and Haas, 1933.

My Next Bride. New York: Smith and Haas, 1934.

Death of a Man. New York: Harcourt, Brace & Company, 1936.

Monday Night. New York: Harcourt, Brace & Company, 1938.

The Crazy Hunter. New York: Harcourt, Brace & Company, 1940. [Three short novels.]

Primer for Combat. New York: Simon and Schuster, 1942.

Avalanche. New York: Simon and Schuster, 1944. (Editions for Armed Services, 1944.)

A Frenchman Must Die. New York: Simon and Schuster, 1946.

1939. New York: Simon and Schuster, 1948.

His Human Majesty. New York: Whittlesey House, 1949.

The Seagull on the Step. New York: Alfred A. Knopf, 1955.

*****Three Short Novels.** Deacon Press, 1950. [Contains two of the three titles found in **Crazy Hunter.**]

Generation Without Farewell. New York: Alfred A. Knopf, 1960.

The Underground Woman. New York: Doubleday & Company, 1975.

SHORT STORIES

Wedding Day and Other Stories. New York: Cape and Smith, 1930. Published in hardback by Books for Libraries, Inc., 1973.

The First Lover and Other Stories. New York: Smith and Haas, 1933.

The White Horses of Vienna and Other Stories. New York: Harcourt, Brace & Company, 1936.

365 Days. New York: Harcourt, Brace & Company, 1936. [365 short stories (many by Kay Boyle) edited by Kay Boyle, Laurence Vail and Nina Conarain.]

The Crazy Hunter. New York: Harcourt, Brace & Company, 1940.

Thirty Stories. New York: Simon and Schuster, 1946. (New Directions, 1957.)

The Smoking Mountain: Stories of Postwar Germany. New York: McGraw-Hill, 1951. Reissued in hardback as **The Smoking Mountain: Stories of Germany During the Occupation**, by Alfred A. Knopf, 1963.

*Published in paperback only.

Nothing Ever Breaks Except the Heart. Garden City: Doubleday & Company, 1966.

NON-FICTION

Breaking the Silence: Why a Mother Tells her Son About the Nazi Era. New York: Institute for Human Relations Press, American Jewish Committee, 1962.

The Long Walk at San Francisco State and Other Essays. New York: Grove Press, 1970. (Evergreen Black Cat, 1970.)

*Enough of Dying: Voices for Peace. Dell, 1972 (a Laurel paperback). [Edited by Kay Boyle and Justine Van Gunday.]

POETRY

*A Statement: For El Greco and William Carlos Williams. Modern Editions Press, pamphlet series 1 number 3, 1932.

A Glad Day. Norfolk: New Directions, 1938.

American Citizen, Naturalized in Leadville, Colorado. New York: Simon and Schuster, 1944.

Collected Poems. New York: Alfred A. Knopf, 1962.

Testament for My Students and Other Poems. Garden City: Doubleday & Company, 1970.

CHILDREN'S BOOKS

The Youngest Camel. Boston: Little, Brown and Company, 1939. [This was extensively rewritten and revised; published by Harper & Row, 1959.]

Pinky the Cat Who Liked to Sleep. New York: Crowell-Collier, 1966.

Pinky in Persia. New York: Crowell-Collier, 1968.

AUTOBIOGRAPHY

Being Geniuses Together, 1920–1930. Garden City: Doubleday & Company, 1968. By Kay Boyle and Robert McAlmon. [This is a re-editing of McAlmon's 1938 book, with chapters by Kay Boyle woven in.]

*Published in paperback only.

OTHER

Joseph Delteil. **Don Juan.** New York: Cape and Smith, 1931. [Translated by Kay Boyle.]

Raymond Radiquet. **Devil in the Flesh.** New York: Harrison Smith, 1932. [Translated by Kay Boyle.]

The Autobiography of Emanuel Carnevali. New York: Horizon Press, 1967. [Compiled by Kay Boyle.]

Don Carpenter

Our interview with Don Carpenter took place in his large second floor flat in San Francisco's Richmond District.

The living room holds comfortable furniture, a stereo, a television, and a built-in bookcase. One shelf is taken up with the American and foreign editions of his books. A large opening leads to a dining room which he uses as an office. A wooden desk with an IBM typewriter on top of it, a long table against the bay windows, and a breakfront on the far wall fill out the room. Everything in the apartment was in order.

Don suggested that we conduct the interview in the kitchen where a long table covered with a checkered cloth stands against one wall. Roger and I sat at either end. Don turned his chair around and sat astride it with his arms resting on its back; we turned on the recorder.

He was eager to talk that day. Wearing an orange sweat shirt, blue jeans and boots he reminded me of Franklin Plover in GETTING OFF, but tougher than Plover. He is quick-minded and answered our questions aggressively. We taped him for two hours, and when I changed the last cassette and was about to put in another, he said, "Enough, enough!"

DT

You mentioned you were trying to decrease your vocabulary, not increase it. Why?

Carpenter: If I can say what I mean with fewer words, more people will understand. Richard Brautigan is into that, too. He has one book that's got, I think, only 750 different words in it. What you want is for the reader to dissolve the language that stands between him and the people he's reading about, so there's no language there at all. Then he's confronted with the actual experience of those people. If little linguistic things stick up, like *fine writing* and stuff like that, then you're suddenly paying attention to the language and not to what the language is supposed to convey. I understand there's a whole branch of fiction whose concerns are linguistic. Mine aren't.

How did you get started as a writer?

Carpenter: I started when I was sixteen years old. I really don't know how, except from that time until the present, I've never had any doubt, or change of mind, or desire to be anything else. It was then that I knew finally and at last and forever that I was not going to be a trumpet player or an actor. I got into writing at Acalanes High School in Walnut Creek where I'd transferred from Berkeley High. I began then the process of private-time reading and private-time writing that's generally the beginning of any writer.

What happened to the trumpet?

Carpenter: Well, there were three. The first one my parents sold. The second one I sold. And the third one I gave to a lunatic asylum in central Oregon. I hope McMurphy got it.

Why did you give up music?

Carpenter: Even though I'm wildly romantic and believe in emotional history rather than real history, I can evaluate reality. And the *Realpolitik* of the situation was that if I ever wanted to be a trumpet player, I'd be nine hundred years old before I even developed a lip. Then we get to the question of, "Can you finger?" I mean, I just wasn't any good at it. No good *at all*.

Why are you a writer?

Carpenter: I'm not only a writer, I'm a professional writer. To quote Paul Goodman, "I only budge for folding money." And that's what a professional is. You don't show your work to people who can't pay for it. That's the difference between an amateur and a professional. I made up my mind years and years ago that I was going to make my living as a writer. So, the answer to your question, "Why are you a writer?" is "Fame and wealth, me boy, fame and wealth." Why is anybody anything?

Are you rich?

Carpenter: No.

Are you famous?

Carpenter: No.

But that is your primary motivation?

Carpenter: It must be. What else could be driving me?

There are a lot of easier ways to be rich and famous.

Carpenter: Oh, yeah. But not for me. You could become notorious; that's easy. Well I'm being slightly facetious, but in entirely the right direction. I think the whole concept of being an artist for art's sake is specious. I don't believe it. I've never met such a person in my life. The fact is I like to spend an enormous amount of time alone. I always have since I was a little tiny kid. And writing is one of the things you can do when you're alone. It had been made clear to me as a child that I would never be able to get along in any kind of social situation as a functional member of any kind of team. I knew that if I was going to make any kind of living, it was going to have to be on my own hook where other people's presence and demands and needs and interests would not affect it. And, of course, the arts immediately pop into mind, because that's exactly what they are. They are the way that private individuals can relate to and belong to society without too much pressure.

Does the necessity to make a living involve any sort of compromise on your part?

Carpenter: No. Unless the bird that pecks on your particular liver is of such a nature that there is never going to be an audience for you, like Beckett. And yet, lo and behold, Beckett is a world-famous writer. A very, very, well-known guy. Makes a lot of dough.

Have all of your books been successful?

Carpenter: Financially, no. But they've done what I wanted them to do. HARD RAIN FALLING made a lot of money. BLADE OF LIGHT and MURDER OF THE FROGS lost a lot of money. They were tied together in the same book contract. GETTING OFF did me the best.

You said that MURDER OF THE FROGS and BLADE OF LIGHT lost money. How did they do what you wanted them to do?

Carpenter: Well, you have to have some realism in your soul somewhere. BLADE OF LIGHT is not an easily accessible story. It's a very complex, extremely literary, highly-compacted story, and a much constructed story. I write very densely. Every word is connected to everything else. And I just knew that there were not going to be a lot of people who cared about this book. But the ones who did really dug it.

I thought it was your best book.

Carpenter: People who like it, really like it. And, man, that's what I want. And MURDER OF THE FROGS is a collection of stories, friends. They do not make money. You are fucking lucky to get them printed and reviewed.

Were they published elsewhere?

Carpenter: No. They are not magazine stories. If you're gonna submit a story to a magazine, it is unrealistic to submit a story that you know they won't print. A magazine has rights, just as an author has rights. The magazine has a right to say, "We will print what we like, and we will ask you to alter it if we don't like it in its present form." And you can alter it or go home. I choose not to do that because there are no magazines in this country that print the kind of stories I write; so it's asinine to send them out. They say, "Yeah, goo, it would be nice to print, but, God, bleaah!" We sold two or three thousand copies, and that's phenomenal for a collection of stories. I mean, that's really good. And so, I'm really very, very happy because that means that it's in a lot of libraries. Shit, that's what I wanted. I want people to read it. And you cannot expect millions of people to read a collection of short stories. They're just not into it. I don't buy collections of short stories, so why should I ask anybody else to?

You seem very positive and very sure of yourself, and you're quite optimistic about your ability to do these things—

Carpenter: Don't forget the word luck.

—but your books are about losers. Why?

Carpenter: There's losing and there's losing. I write about the people I write about, because they're the only people who interest me.

Could you generalize about some of the things you are saying in your work? Is there some underlying theme in your work?

Carpenter: No. Primarily, I'm a storyteller. I agree with B. Traven, whom I consider to be one of our finest writers, that it is better to tell a good story to a lot of people than to tell a "great" story to a few people. Did you see the full blown SEVEN SAMURAI, the three-and-one-half-hour version? It takes an hour and a half to pick the seven, and the reason it takes an hour and a half, before the adventure starts, is because Kurosawa is making what's going on accessible to the most ignorant, most illiterate person in Japan. You can watch that as I did when they showed it on Channel Nine. Turn the sound off entirely, and there's not one point that you miss. Because he makes sure that you see every relationship, every necessity, every plot point. It's there, and it's accessible to you. But, at the same time, Kurosawa and Traven and I know that you're only gonna keep their attention for that hour and a half picking the seven if what you're showing is exciting. Now, exciting is a funny word. You have to excite the emotions of your viewer and your reader. There are a lot of cheap ways to do this. And, if you're technically proficient, you will not use those cheap ways. You will use more proficient ways.

The cheapest way in the world to attract attention is to pull a gun out and fire it, and that's how most of them do it. "Well, let's see. We'll write about the police because you know there are screaming cars, bang, bang, blood, and good guys, and bad guys." See? But that's like, if you were in the food business, selling junk food to people, because you know they'll eat it, not because you know it's good for them. I don't want to sell junk food. I want to sell health-food sandwiches. You know, when a book like Jacqueline Suzanne's LOVE MACHINE comes out, you say, "Oh, I don't want those readers." But you really would like to reach those people. There is nobody that you really wouldn't like to reach with your work. You *take it down*. That's what I mean by reducing your vocabulary. You can take certain things down, but certain things like *what* you're writing about, you can never alter. It's your view of the way things really are, and you're stuck with it. That you must never compromise. Never, ever, ever.

And what is your view of the way things really are?

Carpenter: Well, you've read the books, you know.

But somebody might read this who would not have read your work and would not know.

Carpenter: Well, the books have to stand for themselves. I can't speak for them. If I was able to express my view of the universe without writing fiction, I would do so. This is what happened to Mailer. He found that he can come out from behind the fictional mask and speak in the first person and receive his audience. He still wants to write novels, but more than anything he wants to address the public. Like Lenny Bruce.

How much of your work is based on personal experience?

Carpenter: None of it. All of it. I believe that fiction is the work of the imagination, not research. So I don't believe in research at all. Ask me specific questions about specific books, and I'll tell you where the material comes from.

Were you ever in jail?

Carpenter: Yes.

Where? Why?

Carpenter: Seaside, Oregon. Overnight. Carrying six cans of beer down the street. Moping with intent to gawk. That's the most jail time I've done. I had never seen San Quentin when I wrote HARD RAIN FALLING. I've been in since. I didn't do anything wrong in the book. I had a friend who told me stories about what was going on in there that I drew from quite strongly. Two friends actually. The main character in BLADE OF LIGHT is a guy I went to school with. I had to fight him my first day in school. It haunted me that I had to be one of the rejectors when I knew so well how he must have felt. He's got calamine lotion all over his face all the time, right? And these tiny, piggy, blue eyes, this pink scummy hair. And you absolutely do not want to look at this guy, yet you realize he's watching you turn away from him. And he's inside there, and he knows he's trapped in there, just as you know you're trapped in here, see? So I put myself into him to see how I would act if I was caught inside this grotesque frame. I mean, you know, we're all caught in this thing. We all wake up at three o'clock in the morning saying, "How am I gonna get out of here? How am I gonna get out of here? Can I start over? Can I do *anything* to be someone else?"

All the incidents in the book happen only as they reflect this guy's character. Everything is invented. Has to be. Because what's important is saying what has to be said about this person. See, the character is everything. You know who your people are and you put them together in whatever magical combinations you can find to put them together.

I imagine that you have been called a naturalist by some people.

Carpenter: Quite often, yes.

How do you react to that?

Carpenter: Well, that's their problem. I'm not into literary criticism at all.

Do you consider your view of life grim, harsh, pessimistic?

Carpenter: I'm an atheist. I don't see any moral superstructure to the universe at all. I consider my work optimistic in that the people, during the period I'm writing about them, are experiencing intense emotion. It is my belief that this is all there is to it. There is nothing beyond this. I think we're trapped, if trapped is the right word, into a world that cares less and less for us as individual units, and creates more and more agony and pain and trouble by considering us as blocks, un-individuals. With varying labels. The keystone story of my career is a story called "Limbo" which is six pages long. In the course of it, a young man who is isolated by his circumstances, as we all are, is offered an intense emotional experience and can't accept it. And that's limbo. The saddest story I ever wrote. The trouble is in things like endings, because only once have I ended at the moment of the experience. That was a story called "One of Those Big City Girls." Usually I like to leave Jack Leavitt sitting in Enrico's drinking a glass of somebody else's whiskey.

And then you shift to a different character. I was going to ask you about that. At the end of BLADE OF LIGHT *you shift from Semple to Rosemary. At the end of* HARD RAIN FALLING *you shift from Jack Leavitt to Myron Bronson and Sally King. In other words, you shift from the main characters to characters who up to now have been only supporting.*

Carpenter: Those are fumbling attempts toward using point of view as a way of seeing a character from different angles. The reason HARD RAIN FALLING ends with Myron Bronson is because he represents the dominant culture in our society, that is to say, the aggressive, Western, independent, wealthy man who sees this man's family, says, "I really must have that family," and takes it. What I wanted to show in that last scene is that he didn't get what he took. What he got was something entirely different. See, the last section is not about him, or her, it's about the kid, the little boy. And how you can't have it all. If Jack has nothing, then Myron has nothing, too. Because if you don't have it all, you're finished.

So then none of us has it all, so none of us has anything?

Carpenter: NO, NO, NO. While Jack was left holding a glass of whiskey in his hand, facing the future, he will survive. Myron Bronson, on the other hand, by having had a vasectomy, and then taking someone else's family to give himself this panache, this position, is really very, very rancid grapes, man. Because if the woman you've got is the woman you've stolen, the next thing you know you turn around and somebody has stolen her. The child you've got is not your own. You suddenly realize, "Hey, that's not my child. That child is a great deal more, or a great deal less, than I am."

What effect do you think this shifting at the end has on the reader?

Carpenter: The writer is a con man, basically, because he's creating an illusion in front of your very eyes, and at the end of that illusion everything goes "pop." Close the book. You're back in a sort of reality. Well, in the con game, there's a thing called "cooling out the mark" that takes place at the end. To keep the sucker from following you around the country wanting his money back. So it's kind of cooling out the reader. I don't want the reader to close the book at the highest emotional point in the book. I want him to have a couple of minutes to regroup his forces. This new book is a much better job of doing that than I've ever done before, because the emotional peak is much closer to the end. Have you read Carlos Baker's biography of Hemingway? The last sentence ends, ". . . and he blew his brains out." But that's a biography of a real person. In fiction you don't want to do an O'Henry and dump the reader in the ocean.

In your stories "Hollywood Heart" and "Hollywood Whore," you are much more sympathetic to Max than to anybody else. Why?

Carpenter: Because Max is the only creator and innovator in those stories, and I chose an old Hollywood studio boss as my character because they created the business. The fact that they created it wrong, or that it's a monster, is a whole other issue. The major metaphor in "Hollywood Whore" is that making movies in Hollywood is like three in the bed, and one of them is a prostitute. You don't really know what your aim is except sexual pleasure, and even that seems a little remote. It seems like something you can just buy. But the point of the main character in "Hollywood Whore" was that he was a hack, not an artist, a man who never considered being an artist. It was never an issue. They are the guys to whom power naturally gravitates, and the story is about his accession to power. He is going to run Hollywood. But Max is the only one of the bunch of people who loved anything. I'm gonna write a whole book about Max called *1938.*

Where did the idea of Max come from?

Carpenter: I got into Max after I found out how Arnold Rothstein's career started. He was the kingpin gambler in the 1920's. He appears in THE GREAT GATSBY as Wolfsheim, the man who fixed the World Series in 1919. Fitzgerald couldn't understand it. Rothstein started out sharking money when he was a little kid. By the time he was twenty, he had an international reputation as a hustler, as a banker, as a tough, tough, dude. Okay, you take that kind of a guy who had grown up in the gutter, and you present him with just a glimmering of the financial possibilities of the movies. And you view him at the same time with the same romantic imagination you yourself have. And you get a guy like Max. Or L. B. Mayer.

So Max is based on a real person?

Carpenter: He's based on all of them. He's L. B. Mayer, who's been very badly treated by history because of Irving Thalberg. He's based on Samuel Goldwyn, a much nicer guy than Max ever was, and he's based on Harry Cohn. All of those guys. I mean, they're really horror shows, those guys. But they saw something. They got caught up in a vision of what movies could be, and I don't know how caught up you've been by the movies, but it's an inexplicable experience. It's a whirlwind. The potential is so gigantic, and what's been done with that potential up to now has been so miniscule. Thank God for television because television made the movies grow up. Television has taken over the function of dispensing junk food. Movies can't get away with junk food anymore. Maybe phenobarbitol from time to time. Television's prime function is to keep the people in their place. They do this by the same message. And the message is: "Don't go for the money. Don't go for the money. Stay with your family. Family values are the real values. People who go after the money are mean people, bad people, ugly people." That's television. The people with all of the money telling the rest of the people not to come after it.

Is everybody in television like that?

Carpenter: No. The intentions of a lot of the people in the business are far, far different. There are a lot of bright, young and not-so-young people in television who have more courage, I think, in fighting their hapless battle of "I'm doing what they want me to do in order to get to a place where I can do what I want to do." I think these people have a lot more courage than the people who are sitting at home saying, "Well, you can't break into the business. You can't be an artist. You can't survive as an artist and break into the business." I think the first thing a writer has to do is risk his integrity, his talent, even his life to do what he wants to do, to take that complete ego trip the artist is always on. You can't say *they* won't let me do it. If you do, you're chicken. Of course they won't let you do it. If they would let you do it, we'd all be doing it, wouldn't we?

You wrote and co-produced the movie PAYDAY. *What's the difference between writing fiction and movies?*

Carpenter: Your intentions in writing a novel are completely different from your intentions in writing a film. The difference goes right to the heart of the fact that a book is meant to be read, and a film script is meant to be obeyed, carried out. See, a book is finished when you're finished writing it. It's really finished. You've got something in your hands. But a screenplay is just a set of instructions to forty technical people. It is technical writing. A movie is not a thing until it is on the screen. And it is forty times more difficult to do than a novel because there are forty people involved, all of whom are craftsmen, by the way. "Craftsman" is my favorite word. And they're all pros, and they're all getting paid really good dough for what they do, which is really—even in our society—a pretty damn good measure of some things.

You mentioned before that you liked to spend a lot of time alone. Is there a conflict in moviemaking?

Carpenter: On the one hand, yes, you want to be home alone, clickity, clickity, clickity, no problems. It's all working beautifully because there's no one to interfere and all that. But, on the other hand, there's a comaraderie in making movies I would not trade for anything.

Why are writers so egotistical? Or are they?

Carpenter: Yes. You have to blow your ego up to match your ambition. Because if your ego won't support your ambition, you're always going to be clunking along wondering if you're worthy of what you're doing. You must never worry whether you're worthy. Now, if you are, in fact, unworthy of what you're doing, you're going to make a colossal fool of yourself. And that's the first thing you've got to admit every morning: "Today I'm going to make a colossal fool of myself." You can't hope to write sentences next to the masters of the English language and still hope to retain some personal sense of dignity. *You can't do it.*

Which writers do you like most?

Carpenter: Alive?

Alive.

Carpenter: Mailer first.

Why Mailer?

Carpenter: He's the best writer around. He risks the most. He is not necessarily the most gifted writer in the country, but he makes the largest effort to use it. Evan Connell. Brautigan.

What do you think of Nabokov?

Carpenter: Well he's talented, but I have no interest in his concerns. I admire him a lot. I like LOLITA and PNIN, I can't read the other stuff. The sky lights up, and the castle is looming over here, and I know that's a mathematical equation for something. I don't want to hear about it.

Let's see, I've got a list of questions here . . .

Carpenter: Let me look at it. (Takes list.) "The style of BLADE OF LIGHT is different from your other books. Is there a reason?" Yes. I was wildly under the influence of Faulkner, and I was trying to write like him.

You have one sentence a page-and-a-half long.

Carpenter: Well, that's a solo. It's evocation of mood through tone. I would take a theme that had to be in there for construction purposes—for example, we have Harold Hunt destroying an automobile, a very finely made automobile, just as he's going to destroy human life. So I get a chance to describe that automobile. So I'm going to do a little Charlie Parker solo on that automobile and evoke all of those automobiles that we all were in love with at the time. So I made a perfect car for me when I was sixteen years old: a 1936 Ford three-window, chopped, with Offenhausers, and twin pipes, and the works, skirts, discs. You don't want short sentences, you know, 1936 Ford. Okay. Three windows. Okay. Painted black. Okay. Spider in the gear shift. Umm humm. You bop. . . . The trick to writing stuff like that is to never rewrite it. Kerouac's phrase is

"Spontaneous bop prosody," and it's a beautiful phrase. And Kerouac was really a master of it.

Would you tell us about GETTING OFF?

Carpenter: Well, this is a very lightweight book. I consider this to be a much more deliberate attempt to be accessible because I wanted people to read it instructively.

Is it autobiographical?

Carpenter: Oh definitely not. That's not my wife, and that's not me, although I rode the high line of fact/fiction quite intensely. I mean, I would steal from my emotions with alacrity. And people would go up to my wife and say, "I feel as if I've known you." And she always has to say, "Well, you don't." As a matter of fact, my ex-wife is a teacher of linguistics.

Was GETTING OFF *a difficult book to write?*

Carpenter: It was extremely painful because I was under a tremendous economic necessity, and I was deliberately using my own life as a focus for the story. I took me about eight months working every day.

Does writing for film and fiction complement each other for you?

Carpenter: Yes, because their intentions are so different. The intention of the novel is internal. Writing movies is a dramatic medium, it's more like cartooning. You have to draw with a little broader stroke. A lot of people think of this as compromising, but if you're going to write for the camera, you must write for the camera, not yourself through the camera. This is why most novelists coming out to Hollywood make bad script writers because they try to bring novelistic concerns to the screenplay. They haven't had the experience of watching their own beautiful words dragging up there on that screen. Once you've seen that. . . . This is where the *High Chaparral* helped me. I wrote an eighteenth-century comedy of manners and sexuality for the *High Chaparral*. It was written to read: "Bipbipbip bipbipbip," and the actors were reading it: "Baaahh! Baaahh"!

How are we gonna type this?

Carpenter: Let's see those questions again. "Most successful book commercially?" GETTING OFF. "What makes a good story or novel?" Your belief that you have a good story or novel to tell is, I think, the primary consideration. This is what I mean by ego. You have to believe it. It's like religion. The priests who don't believe have the hardest lives. "The physical process of writing?" Very exhausting.

Do you work in the morning?

Carpenter: Yes, I have a daily minimum of a thousand words when I'm working. That takes me an hour usually.

And you write a thousand words in an hour?

Carpenter: Yeah. I write very fast. However, you understand that's three hundred and sixty-five thousand words a year of which maybe eighty thousand get printed. The rest of them get thrown out. I consider it a great day if I can throw out forty pages. I don't have to write my thousand words if I've thrown out forty pages.

Do you do a lot of revising?

Carpenter: Oh yes, and I throw out whole sections and rewrite without reference to the previous writing.

Why without reference?

Carpenter: Well, it goes back to bopping. I feel that if it doesn't seem to work, I throw it out and try a different tone. I know the information I want to convey. The information is the least important thing in writing to me.

Do you draft out a plot outline?

Carpenter: Nooooo!

How do you begin a book?

Carpenter: I wish I knew! I always begin with sentences that never end up in the book. Take, for example, the book I've just finished. Janis Joplin's death shook me up. I mean it rattled me. And

I was thinking, "But she's ugly, she's ugly; I mean, she should never have gone into show business in the first place." You could predict it just by looking at her. So the sentence I wrote down was: "She was a very ugly little girl; she should never have gone into show business." I kept that sentence in my head for a year, walking around and thinking bout it. And then another sentence by her mother coming out after she had seen her in a movie and saying. "She was good." Between those two things, the tone arrived. The moment came when I hit the tone. And I thought, "Okay, I'm gonna take it when she's fifteen and when she's thirty-five." Neither sentence actually appears in the book.

What's it called?

Carpenter: THE TRUE LIFE STORY OF JODY MCKEEGAN.

What does it take to be a good writer?

Carpenter: Luck. Talent. Energy. Love. Loneliness. Madness. And the ability to throw your entire life away for what you want. Courage, in short. It takes everything. It takes everything it takes to be a good anything, and more, because it takes that very special ability and overwhelming need to corner people and tell them a story. And you have to do it all the time. It has to be your constant dream and desire. In order to make your dreams come true—and this is what we're really talking about—you have to be careful not to dream for too little. Because if you dream for too little and your dream comes true, you're finished.

NOVELS

Hard Rain Falling. New York: Harcourt, Brace & World, 1964. (Fawcett Crest, 1965.)

Blade of Light. New York: Harcourt, Brace & World, 1967. (Avon Books, 1972.)

Getting Off. New York: E. P. Dutton, 1971. (Pocket Books, 1972.)

The True Life Story of Jody McKeegan. New York: E. P. Dutton, 1975.

SHORT STORIES

Murder of the Frogs and Other Stories. New York: Harcourt, Brace & World, 1969.

Evan S. Connell, Jr.

Our interview with Evan S. Connell, Jr. took place on two separate occasions. The first was in his apartment at Polk and Union Streets. The apartment was orderly and sparsely furnished. Several board and cement block bookcases held his books. On the top shelves he displayed his collection of pre-Columbian sculptures. A photograph of a female nude by Ruth Bernhard, a figurative painting Connell had made several years earlier and prints hung on the walls. His writing table stood in the window facing a view of the Golden Gate Bridge and the Marin hills.

Connell is a tall, imposing figure. He is reserved and serious and gives the impression that he will not speak unless he has something important to say. He responded to our questions directly and without elaboration. He has no theories about writing or intellectualizations about his craft. "I want to exemplify," he told us. During his interview he didn't want us to use a tape recorder, so we had to take down his responses in a hasty scrawl. Recomposing the interview later, we discovered that we didn't have enough material and planned to see him again.

At the time of our second meeting he had finished writing THE CONNOISSEUR and had moved to a large modern apartment in Mill Valley. He prefers Marin County to the city because it's quieter and the air is better, but he complained that the apartment was too dark, and he didn't like the place. His board and cement block bookcases, the sculptures and the pictures were familiar to us in the new surroundings. His same writing desk was placed in front of the bedroom window which had the best view in the apartment.

This time we brought a stenographer friend who helped record his answers. We asked some of the same questions we had asked before, added several and expanded our material.

DT

Do you remember when you first wanted to be a writer?

Connell: Not really. I come from the Midwest. The important thing was a good job and a family. Sons grew up and went into their fathers' businesses. It's not that art and writing were held in contempt; they were just ignored. Thomas Hart Benton lived nearby, and people were aware that he was a famous artist of some kind, but they didn't give it much thought. That was one good thing that came out of the war. People were uprooted and placed in a barracks where there was a certain amount of free time to sit around and wonder, "If I get out of this alive, what am I going to do with my life?"

How did you start writing?

Connell: Fortunately, I had the G. I. Bill. I went back to college and took courses I wanted to take—I wasn't interested in an advanced degree because I didn't think they were any use unless you wanted to teach—and the courses turned out to be in writing and art. I just started sending out stories and getting back rejection slips.

What kept you going?

Connell: Well, I got very discouraged. You have to keep going. Some people only allow themselves a certain amount of time—say three years. I never went along with that.

Why did you choose writing as a career as opposed to art?

Connell: I liked painting better than writing, but I saw a chance of making a living as a writer. Poets and graphic artists are at the bottom of the pole. Writers are only one step up, but at least there's a chance of making a living. I don't think a painter stands a chance without another job like teaching. And there certainly are dangers if you start working at a regular job. You adopt a certain standard of living and come to depend on that paycheck every month; your real work suffers. I was always careful to take work that I didn't consider permanent: hauling ice, things like that. The worst job I ever had was with the California Department of Unemployment where I interviewed unemployed laborers all day.

In THE PATRIOT, *Melvin returns from the war and gets involved with abstract expressionism. Later, he rejects it. What is your feeling about it?*

Connell: I'm suspicious of abstract expressionism. It's like a ball game with no rules. The early abstract expressionists put in a long apprenticeship; they could do other things as well. This has been forgotten. The newer ones ignore craftsmanship. It's too easy. I'm skeptical because it's too personal; there's no objective way of evaluating it.

Could you comment on the relationship between personal experience and imagination in your own work? Were MRS. BRIDGE *and* MR. BRIDGE *autobiographical in some way?*

Connell: If you never draw from personal experience it seems to me that the book loses a feeling of authenticity. Though there are exceptions. David Stacton, I'm told, never visited Japan, but his

Japan is thoroughly convincing. Bellow's Africa in HENDERSON is, to me, utterly unconvincing—which is what usually happens.

In the two BRIDGE books, how much came from my own parents, from friends and people I knew, and from my imagination, I really don't know. All those things fuse together after awhile, and it's really hard to separate them. In one sense they were easy books to write because I could remember what that kind of life was like. I had my own childhood perceptions to fall back on. THE DIARY OF A RAPIST was much harder. I was never sure whether I was right, but with the BRIDGE books I could tell just by looking at them.

Where did the idea for THE DIARY OF A RAPIST *come from?*

Connell: Two things, I believe. One, a number of years ago, about fifteen years ago, Miss California was raped twice by the same man. It was so strange it stayed in my mind. Also, in reading the newspapers, I noticed that someone was being raped almost every day. I realized that nothing serious had been written about rape, and it interested me, especially because of its prevalence and its lack of treatment in fiction. Then, I went to the library and looked under "Rape." I found "The Rape of the Lock" and "The Rape of Lucrece," but strangely little about plain old American rape. There's something farcical about Miss California parading around in a bathing suit and doing things to some little man. He raped her twice and is doing time for it in Quentin. He's still there.

Why does the rapist go back the second time?

Connell: Penitential, he feels guilty, he loves her. The guy in Quentin went back to the beauty queen, but the second time he raped her, he took her home afterward and was caught. Why did he drive her home? The only sense I can make of it was that he loved her. It's an example of America's incredible romanticism. A Frenchman, or any European, would never have taken her home afterward. This insane romanticism seems to me to be singularly American.

Obviously, you couldn't rely on personal experience in writing this book. Yet Earl Summerfield is totally convincing. . . .

Connell: A friend of mine in L. A. who is a psychiatrist helped me with the book. He had access to some information and some police files. I also read what I could, which was precious little. I also talked with several women who had been raped, or almost raped, and tried to get as much information as possible on how the man behaved and what he said and the impression he made on them.

Would you mind discussing your working habits?

Connell: I work essentially a nine-to-five day, seven days a week, and then take off when I can't stand it any more. I do a lot of rewriting. In THE PATRIOT, I rewrote one chapter fourteen or fifteen times.

Was that the chapter where Melvin takes his last flight?

Connell: How did you know?

It's the high point of the book. It doesn't seem that anyone unfamiliar with flying could have written that chapter.

Connell: After graduating from Pensacola I was sent to New Orleans to an instructors' training school, after which I was assigned to the Glenview Naval Air Station outside Chicago as a flight instructor. Technically, THE PATRIOT is the least successful book I've done. I haven't read it in years. It's undigested. I couldn't figure out what to do with it. I wrote it six times.

Could you put your finger on what went wrong?

Connell: I can't really. . . . It just seems clumsy; it seems to break in half. The experience was still too vivid for me to have much critical sense about what I was doing. I think that happens often with a very powerful experience. This is not really a good story because the facts never quite metamorphosed or crystalized into fiction.

How do you write about a powerful experience successfully then?

Connell: You have to have a certain objective control and distance. Sometimes chronological distance can do it. At other times you see more objectively by changing the sex of the central character. Sometimes you change the locale. You try different things to achieve a more comprehensive view. I don't think there's a simple way of doing it.

But the powerful experience is necessary?

Connell: Yes, it makes all the difference. Without it, a book doesn't work at all. If you go to museums you can see the importance of a powerful feeling. Very often, you'll see an original sketch next to the finished painting, and sometimes the painting is inferior. It's just too perfect. It lacks something the sketch had. Some of the feeling has been eroded.

Maybe what we're talking about is that thing called "inspiration."

Connell: I'm not sure what that word means, but there are times a story exceeds the bounds you planned for it and seems to be exceeding those bounds in an organic way. That's one of the things you hope for. You work by trial and error. If you get the first sentence just right, you can go on. I guess what all this means is the conscious and unconscious join forces in a technically combined piece of work. You have to have the powerful feeling, and you also have to have the control.

What's your opinion of Nabokov's work?

Connell: He's brilliant and facile. He can write a book on Saturday afternoon just by turning off his head and turning on his fingers. But when you finish reading, everything is gone ten minutes later. I read TRANSPARENT THINGS, and there's nothing there. If he's personally involved and allows his feelings to work along with that tremendous facility, he writes something like LOLITA, a modern classic.

You said you did a lot of rewriting. Do you spend a lot of time looking for the mot juste?

Connell: (Laughing) The what? Sure, I use a thesaurus a lot. Some things are worth working for. Everyone has two vocabularies: a recognition vocabulary and a speaking vocabulary. It's not a matter of intentionally using obscure words, but of using the appropriate word that works. Sometimes, the word that says what you want to say best belongs to the recognition vocabulary rather than the spoken one.

Does looking for the right word slow down the flow of the narration?

Connell: No, I do so much revising there's plenty of time to go back after the first draft. I'll use an approximation and make a note in the margin. Sometimes you discover there's no word that fits. Then it helps to rewrite the sentence. I've never had a sentence turn up in the final form as it was in the beginning.

That sounds like an incredible amount of work. When do you decide to stop revising?

Connell: Obviously, you can go on more or less indefinitely making minor improvements. I stop when I find I've changed a comma to a semicolon and then back to a comma. It's just a slow business to find a better way to say what you have in mind. Writing is less immediate than the graphic arts, but it's similar because your work never turns out quite as well as you hope it will. That's why you keep doing it.

Since your first book, do you find that you've become more critical of your work and that each successive book is more difficult?

Connell: I'm more critical, but in a way I think the work is easier, partly because I can draw on previous problems. The longer you work on anything, the more technical devices you have at hand. I know this was true with POINTS FOR A COMPASS ROSE. I had been through the whole thing before with NOTES FROM A BOTTLE FOUND ON THE BEACH AT CARMEL. I could remember where I was stuck on the first book, and it simplified work on the second.

How has your style evolved since THE PATRIOT?

Connell: I don't know. Every story you work on seems to require a different style. I try to find what is appropriate. I would hope my style is more evocative and more precise. I would hope it is. . . .

How do you know when the style is appropriate, when you have it right?

Connell: You feel it. When you fly a light plane without using any instruments, you feel it in the seat of your pants. If you hit a baseball well, you feel it all the way through.

How did you arrive at the particular form or style you used in MRS. BRIDGE?

Connell: MRS. BRIDGE was turned down by six or eight publishers. They were afraid of the form. I tried to write it the conventional way, but I couldn't force what were essentially paragraphs into chapters twenty pages long. The idea of titling those individual paragraphs probably came when I titled them for myself as I was arranging them. The original idea of the titles may have come from MOBY DICK. Sometimes the form never develops. One little story I have had in mind for years. Maybe tomorrow I'll find the right form.

Mrs. Bridge is shallow, but somehow you make her a sympathetic character—maybe because she's always been protected, and it's not her fault—but you seem to be more severe with Mr. Bridge.

Connell: Sure, I considered him to be much more conscious of the world around him. You judge people by their capacity. If a man is a hack writer, you don't bother with him, but if he's capable and writes a bad book, you come down hard on him. I reviewed Capote's IN COLD BLOOD for the CHRONICLE and gave it a bad review because I thought he could do better than that.

Both Mr. and Mrs. Bridge have moments of illumination, but don't act on their moments of awareness. They're not tragic characters in the classic sense. Do you think tragedy is possible in the modern world?

Connell: Sure, it happens all the time. Those guys who stole the Pentagon Papers stuck their necks out. They were heroes for the moment, and they suffered for it. We're surrounded by tragedy. We're in the middle of it right now. The reason the Bridges don't act on their discoveries is that it wouldn't be them.

Mr. and Mrs. Bridge are so real they're almost models of the Midwestern upper-middle class. Was this intentional?

Connell: I think you always try to do that. There's a half-conscious hope that if you find the essence of a character, the character will become a model.

Your stories about Southerners seem very true to the way those people act and speak. Have you lived in the South?

Connell: I was faking it. I was depending on guide books for colloquial expressions. I had spent a couple of years in parts of the South, but I didn't feel familiar with it. And my family is from the Midwest by way of the South. There doesn't seem to be too much difference.

You've also written some non-fiction. In I AM A LOVER *you selected the quotes to accompany a series of photographs. They're remarkable because they seem to capture the essence of the photograph and also reflect your own point of view. How did you go about selecting the quotes?*

Connell: It took quite a lot longer than I thought it would. When I began, I thought it might take two or three weekends. I was quite methodical. I went all the way through BARTLETT'S QUOTATIONS, and that's quite a job.

You read all of BARTLETT'S QUOTATIONS?

Connell: Yes. There are probably only three people who've done it: Bartlett, the editor, and myself. I also went through a number of other books.

How did you know when you found a quote you could use?

Connell: Some of them would come to mind immediately, and I marked them. I went through all kinds of books just marking possible quotations to use. Mostly, it was just trial and error.

Are there any writers you particularly respect?

Connell: Chekhov, Tolstoy, Mann, and I have considerable respect for de Maupassant; even though he's not that deep, he had a great technical facility for producing the effect he wanted. I've read a whole string of Russian writers, including Turgenev, Andreyev and some others. Also, Coppard, who was one of the better English writers, even though you don't hear that much about him.

One of your characters, Muhlbach, says, "Today's authors seem tortured, frenetic, and shallow, empty of fond; say that they do not know how to write of the world and its magic, but merely of themselves; say that they are, in a word, tiresome." Do you think this is true of modern writers, particularly American writers?

Connell: Yes, that about says it. I don't read much fiction. I almost never read contemporary novels. I wait several years and see if they hold up. I've read all of Styron and like his work, and Mailer, in spite of his wild variations—or maybe because of them. Thomas Mann once pointed out that the Europeans have a more consistent qualitative level than we do. The Europeans seem to have something we lack. Perhaps it's the unsettled nature of the United States.

I read a lot of non-fiction: archeological, anthropological, historical. The overtones are often so much greater than in fiction. They've recently found some Viking cemeteries in Greenland. The skeletons were almost dwarfs. Apparently they were suffering from rickets and malnutrition, but when the European ships came in, they had to have the latest European fashions. They were practically starving to death, but were dressed in the latest styles. You can go through a three-hundred-page novel and never find anything as substantial as that. Of course, you can find it in Tolstoy or Melville, but there aren't many of them around.

NOTES FROM A BOTTLE FOUND ON THE BEACH AT CARMEL *and* POINTS FOR A COMPASS ROSE *seem to be full of things like that.*

Connell: In the course of reading over the years, I underlined things which I thought were interesting. I wrote NOTES as an experimental short story and considered that the end of it. Every now and then someone would read it and seem interested. One time I ran into George Hitchcock at the Buena Vista Cafe, and he wondered if it could be expanded into a book, so then I decided to do it. Viking was terrified of it. They couldn't figure out what it was.

They didn't want to print it. It probably wouldn't have been printed if it hadn't been published in CONTACT first which made it possible for Viking to use the original plates.

Did you alter the material you found and underlined?

Connell: It depends. If I were quoting something or if it were specific history, I didn't. Under some circumstances, I might have given a different interpretation or used a variation. I got a lot of material from two books: Robert Burton's THE ANATOMY OF MEL- ANCHOLY and Paul Herrmann's CONQUEST BY MAN.

The books seem to be a strange mixture of history, religion, philosophy, human brutality. We couldn't figure them out.

Connell: I was putting everything into the books I thought appropriate. I wanted to make them as complex as possible. I like things that can't be solved; I think that makes the best work. You can't touch bottom with the greatest writers. If you read enough Hawthorne, you touch bottom, you see what he's doing, but not Melville. I've read some of Chekhov's stories over and over and can't get to the bottom of him. With the greatest writers there's this sense of limitless depth.

Besides this depth is there another way of determining whether a book is great?

Connell: I suppose it depends on how long you remember the book.

Do you have any ideas on how to make a book memorable?

Connell: I wish I knew. I don't know. I'm not avoiding the question. Whatever is in the writer. The magic moment when you hit something solid. How that solidity is achieved or why it emanates from a book, I don't know.

In NOTES you mention a number of different lattitudes and longitudes for the ship before it sinks. Does it go anywhere?

Connell: No, I just checked a map to make sure it wasn't on land. Ken Lamott was very concerned about that. He spent a lot of time trying to chart the course of the ship. The book is an abstract mosaic. People get distressed. They say you can't understand it. You aren't supposed to understand it. If it moves you, fine. If it doesn't, forget it.

One of the people we've talked to said that many writers give up striving for the large conception which is valuable in itself.

Connell: That's a good comment. That's what I tried to do in NOTES and POINTS FOR A COMPASS ROSE. I suppose they're my favorite books for that reason.

Which one do you prefer?

Connell: POINTS FOR A COMPASS ROSE.

Why?

Connell: My editor Bob Gottlieb said—I can't recall exactly—something to the effect that NOTES was a book struggling to find its form and that POINTS FOR A COMPASS ROSE had found its form. I agree.

It seems to be a darker book than NOTES.

Connell: Darker. . . . Some people have said that. Maybe it seems darker because of the things that have been happening in the past couple of years.

Can you generalize about what you want to get across in your work?

Connell: No.

Do you think of yourself as a storyteller or as a writer of ideas?

Connell: I've never thought about it until now. I try to find out how to exemplify.

Do you consider yourself a realist, a romantic, a prophet?

Connell: I don't know. I try to find the best form for what I'm doing. I don't care what it's called.

How did you arrive at the form for NOTES and POINTS FOR A COMPASS ROSE?

Connell: So many things happen that stick with you. And yet, they don't have enough substance for a story or novel. They're just complete in themselves. With this kind of book you can make use of those things.

Do you prefer this type of thing or novels or short stories?

Connell: I like to do these very, very short things. I have always had trouble constructing a fifteen chapter novel.

You've written a number of short stories that have been collected in two books. Are there any others?

Connell: Oh yeah, quite a few more. They don't always sell. Sometimes the agency sends back a story after ten years of going around the magazines. They always go to THE NEW YORKER first and wind up in a quarterly making twenty-five bucks or something.

Where did that outrageous story about Henrietta* come from?

Connell: It was told to me by Max Steele in Paris. It was told to him by Theodora Keogh. It was supposed to have happened. I told Max that if he didn't write it, I was going to. I gave him a year. He didn't use it, and I did. Ever since, he's been threatening to sue me.

Do you have a favorite story?

Connell: Probably "Saint Augustine's Pigeon." It was sent to THE SATURDAY EVENING POST. They wanted to cut out the end where the pigeon destroys Muhlbach. Of course, that was the whole point. They thought it wasn't very nice. They were quite right.

You've written four long stories about Muhlbach. How did you originally get the idea for him?

Connell: He comes from "Disorder and Early Sorrow" by Thomas Mann. Some stories are touchstones for me. I think the first Muhlbach story was sent to THE PARIS REVIEW. Plimpton said he felt he was reading "Disorder and Early Sorrow" over again. Then, it was published by Ray West in THE WESTERN REVIEW. He recognized

*"The Short Happy Life of Henrietta" collected in AT THE CROSSROADS AND OTHER STORIES the indebtedness to Mann, but thought it functioned on its own merits.

So, in addition to imagination and personal experience, you've used other writers as a stimulus to your own work?

Connell: You use everything you can. I was in North Beach one evening. I was dressed up and a pigeon got me. It looked like epaulets on my coat, and my evening was wiped out. I was reading St. Augustine's CONFESSIONS at the time, and the indignity of being shit upon by a pigeon and St. Augustine came together with the character Muhlbach. The result is "Saint Augustine's Pigeon." That's just one example. It's a deliberate search from both art and life for those elements which magically come together. I think you get your best things out of life, but if you have a sense you're reading about the author, it's less than great. When Tolstoy writes about life in the army barracks, you get a sense of that life and not autobiography.

We both thought Muhlbach was complex and interesting. Do you plan a novel about him?

Connell: Before I would have said he was only suitable for long stories, but I've just finished a 225-page manuscript about him, and I don't think I can get away with calling it a story.

What is the new book going to be called when it's published?

Connell: THE CONNOISSEUR.

One last question: do you believe a writer is many people, a man who uses many masks?

Connell: Sounds like a romantic idea. I'll try it sometime.

NOVELS

Mrs. Bridge. New York: The Viking Press, 1959. (Dell, 1960; Viking Compass, 1963; Fawcett Premier, 1970, 1974.)

The Patriot. New York: The Viking Press, 1960. (Pacific Coast Publishers—A Farallon Book, 1967.)

The Diary of a Rapist. New York: Simon and Schuster, 1966. (Dell, 1967.)

Mr. Bridge. New York: Alfred A. Knopf, 1969. (Fawcett Premier, 1970.)

The Connoisseur. New York: Alfred A. Knopf, 1974.

Double Honeymoon. New York: G. P. Putnam's Sons, 1976.

SHORT STORIES

The Anatomy Lesson and Other Stories. New York: The Viking Press, 1957. (Pacific Coast Publishers—A Farallon Book, 1969.)

At the Crossroads. New York: Simon and Schuster, 1965.

POETRY

Notes From a Bottle Found on the Beach at Carmel. New York: The Viking Press, 1963. (Pacific Coast Publishers—A Farallon Book, 1969.)

Points For a Compass Rose. New York: Alfred A. Knopf, 1973.

OTHER

I am a Lover. Sausalito, California: Contact Editions, 1961. [Photography by Jerry Stoll; comments selected from various sources by Evan S. Connell, Jr.] (Pacific Coast Publishers—A Farallon Book, 1961.)

*Woman by Three. Pacific Coast Publishers—A Farallon Book, 1969. [Photography by Joanne Leonard, Michael Bry and Barbara Cannon Myers; text selected by Evan S. Connell, Jr.]

*Published only in paperback.

Alfred Coppel

Alfred Coppel lives with his wife Elisabeth in a modest, contemporary house in Palo Alto. A bright red Alfa Romeo, his favorite automobile (which he sometimes gives to the central character in his novels) stands in his carport.

His writing room reveals his fascination for machines. Strung from the ceiling are model airplanes of different vintages. He owns three Olympia typewriters: an electric, a manual portable, and a manual standard. A telephone answering machine takes his calls when he is away or at work.

On one wall he keeps the American, European and Asian editions of the sixteen novels he has published, three under the pseudonym "A. C. Marin" and three others as "Robert Gilman." On another wall he displays the dustjackets of his novels mounted on cardboard.

In person, Coppel doesn't give the impression of a man of action. He is of medium height and a casual dresser. He is quiet, somewhat reserved, perhaps shy. Yet his biography shows that he was a pilot during World War II, he still flies light aircraft, and once raced sports cars. Since the success of his recent novel, THIRTY-FOUR EAST, he owns a 27' Santa Cruz sailboat and on weekends competes in races on San Francisco Bay.

During the interview he leaned back at his desk with his feet propped up on the typewriter stand. His answers to our questions were direct and complete, suggesting that he had thought a lot about his working methods in the same careful, logical manner that he thinks through each of his novels.

DT

In the Fifties you wrote two books: HERO DRIVER *and* NIGHT OF FIRE AND SNOW. *Since 1960, you have written fourteen. That's a fictional explosion. What happened?*

Coppel: In the early Fifties I was more interested in sports car racing than I was in constructive work. But the sporting scene was so fertile it did encourage me to write about it, and so I did. The result was HERO DRIVER. It took me thirty days to write it. It was published by Crown. It is a rough and rather clumsily constructed book, but it isn't bad. At least it is a true picture of what that life was like at that time.

And NIGHT OF FIRE AND SNOW?

Coppel: Another rough one. By that I mean the mechanisms and devices show, and the plot creaks a bit. But maybe that's to be expected in a second novel. Anyway, I wrote it and took off for Europe thinking I could do more work there. You see, I was beginning to worry about what I was going to do with my life. I had inherited a fairly large sum of money from my father, but what with racing and helling around, it was going fast. Besides, I really wanted to be a novelist—not a sports car racer. So we took off for Europe in the hope I could write there. . . .

And did you write?

Coppel: Hell, no. Europe may be fine for some writers, but I am no expatriate. I had a grand old time, but I didn't get a lick of work done. Oh, all that I saw and did in that year abroad surfaced in later work, but while I was there I never settled down to work. There was too much to see and do.

You came back to the states in 1957 then.

Coppel: That's right. And by 1958 I still hadn't written anything more—except a few short stories—and the money was gone. My two books hadn't made any real money, so there was only one thing to do. Get a job. The trouble was, I didn't know how. I had to learn while doing, you might say. It's pretty damned difficult to walk into a place and ask for work and have those strictly-by-the-book people in personnel ask you where you last worked, and you have to tell them: "I've never had a job." They look at you like something weird, believe me. Thirty-eight years old and never held any sort of job? Unless you count the Air Force, you have to say, "That's right. But I can do whatever you want done—honest." What you really mean is that you need the money badly and you'll give them your best efforts. It takes time to find anyone who will hire you under those conditions. And having published two novels doesn't impress personnel people very much, let me tell you. It even makes them a little resentful. They asked me for resumes, and I didn't know what a resume was or what it was for. Anyway, I finally got on as a proposal's writer for Philco Western Development Laboratories. They were working on communications satellites. Maybe the fact I'd written science fiction helped. My job was to take what the engineers wrote and translate it into language a non-engineer could understand. I held that job for almost a year —despite the fact that my supervisor kept trying to get rid of me by telling me how "over-qualified" I was. Hell, I knew I was over-qualified, but I needed the four hundred and twenty dollars a month I was getting. Then I went to work for a public relations firm. I thought I'd like it, and when I got the offer I grabbed it. It meant more money—not much more, but some—and I thought it would be a less restricting sort of job. But it was pretty bad. My boss was terrified of antagonizing his clients—and anything new seemed to arouse antagonism. On the side, he put me to work rewriting his books. He fancied himself a writer and his stuff was pretty bad. He needed the attention of a bonehead English teacher, not a professional writer. But he was my boss, and I tried. The book was subsequently published—rather quietly—so I guess what I did helped. Then I quit and started my own agency. I'd managed to finish DARK DECEMBER during this period and it was published in 1960. But I still wasn't working freely. I was too tied-up personally and too hooked on what unemployed writers like to call "the rat race." That is, earning enough money to keep on eating. All during the time I tried to keep my agency going, I was reworking my first really good novel, A CERTAINTY OF LOVE. When that was published, in 1966, and after it was taken in England for a good advance, I decided the time had come to make a choice. Either I was going to be a novelist or I wasn't. I decided to turn pro. A CERTAINTY OF LOVE was published in this country by Harcourt. It made a definite change in my life. I had a fine editor—I still have him—and some assurance that I had a publisher for my next book. I guess I scared hell out of my wife, but I quit the agency I'd gone to after closing down my own, and started writing again. I wasn't sorry to leave the so-called security of an agency job. Any sane man has to hate a thing as phony as advertising and public relations. And I felt so liberated, the work just flowed. I wrote and wrote, and I haven't stopped since then. I've slowed up a bit, but at least I know what it is that I do. I write novels.

You have worked in advertising and public relations, but you have never taught. Why?

Coppel: I have no degree. I left Stanford in my junior year to join the Air Corps and never went back. And I sincerely believe that writing can't be taught. Either you are a writer or you are not. No one can teach you to be one. There are mountains of talent around. Talent is cheap, but writing takes talent *plus* devotion, dedication—call it whatever you will. Discipline. That's a dirty word these days, but there it is. Without self-discipline you can't write. And no one can teach that. There is one other thing. I don't believe writers belong in universities. I know there are plenty of them skulking in academia, but they cripple themselves when they do that. Sinecures are poison for creative people. Give a writer a steady salary, and you ruin him. Keep him in a cloistered school atmosphere, and you castrate him. He sits around, and he talks. He doesn't write. Or if he does, he writes little things, small pieces about small people.

Earlier you mentioned that your latest book, THIRTY-FOUR EAST, *has been better received in Europe than here at home. Why do you think this is so?*

Coppel: American critics tend to be snobs. If a book is not an exercise in navel-contemplation, or if it is ideologically out of step with the current cant, they tend to denigrate it.

In what way do you mean "ideologically out of step?"

Coppel: I'll give you an example. James Gould Cozzens is a fine writer. He has written a series of books about his time, his generation. Fifteen years ago, critics raved about his books. When he published MORNING, NOON AND NIGHT a few years back, in the middle of the Now Generation's temper tantrum, they ripped him to ribbons—for being old, I think, for being out of step with the Youth Culture. Yet his book was of a piece with everything else he has done, good solid work that will be read and reread a hundred years from now. THIRTY-FOUR EAST has appeared in a time of transition. The pacifist delusion is fading a bit, and so the toughness of some of the attitudes expressed in the book got by, and many critics gave it good notices. But it is still a book that has some grit in it, and there is action, too. Academic critics—and most of our critics are academics in spirit if not in fact—aren't really entranced by action novels. Europeans look at things differently. In Europe, THIRTY-FOUR EAST is being reviewed as a serious novel rather than as just another thriller.

Which American writers have affected your work?

Coppel: O'Hara, Faulkner and Hemingway. Hemingway was God to my generation of writers. Though I suspect he'd be cut to ribbons by modern critics. Still he changed the creative map of America.

How did THIRTY-FOUR EAST *begin?*

Coppel: It was conceived a long time ago. I wrote a book called THE GATE OF HELL about the 1956 Arab-Israeli War some years back. That was probably the beginning. I saw how unsatisfactorily that war ended and began wondering about a more permanent solution. By that I mean a peace that might last ten, fifteen, twenty years. Since there was no prospect of the lions and the lambs lying down together in sweet amity, I looked for something else. Something pragmatic. That's how the "Cyprus Accord" of the book came to be written. I wrote the treaty, envisioned it enforced by the only powers who could enforce it—the U. S. and the Soviet Union—and that set the scene. Americans and Russians, nose to nose over a demilitarized zone. The subplots came out of the politics of the Sixties and early Seventies. I'm fascinated by pacifistic liberals— what I call the "McGovern Syndrome": "*Beg and ye shall receive.*" Well, life isn't like that, and I wanted to show, in novelistic terms, what could happen to a pacifist liberal confronted by the bloody *fact* of violence. After all, it was peace-seeking men who probably precipitated World War II by failing to face reality in places like the Rhineland and Munich. The novel coalesced around those major concerns of mine.

In THIRTY-FOUR EAST *there are many characters, and you shift viewpoint from one to another within a close time frame. Is this intended to heighten suspense?*

Coppel: Yes, exactly that.

How did you come up with this technique?

Coppel: It isn't original. It is used by many authors. But it serves the purpose in this particular story—one in which there is both great complexity and a need for swift pace. There is much antecedant material that must be fed into the narrative, yet one can't allow the pace to flag, or the reader will grow restless. So I injected the information into a series of short staccato scenes. This requires a multiple point of view and an almost cinematic style. The pace is varied by lengthening or shortening the scenes, and each scene is made to contain a specific necessary piece of information. For example, the triggor is cocked for the scene of the Vice President's ambush by an earlier scene describing the place where the ambush will take place—a valley between two hills which are compared to the breasts of a reclining woman. In another scene, I mention that the convoy is almost at that place, and the suspense is heightened by something taking place off scene, thousands of miles away. What is actually utilized is a series of small hooks and shocks that bring the reader along, expecting something to happen.

Then you write with the reader consciously in mind?

Coppel: Absolutely. Without a reader a book is just so much print, paper and binding. A reader makes it all come together.

Did you develop this concern for the reader over a period of time, or is it natural to you?

Coppel: It has certainly become second nature to me. I visualize, then write about what I see. I have come to understand that what captured my attention will capture the reader's, will entertain him. Now, many novelists claim they don't care about entertaining their readers. They prefer to instruct, to shock, to preach. I believe that the primary purpose of fiction is to create a mental world the reader can inhabit. That, to my mind, is the heart of the matter. First entertain the reader—then if you insist, shock him, moralize, do what you like. But entertain him all the while, or you'll lose him. I personally will not read a work that fails to entertain me. I will not read what bores me—no matter how elevating the content.

You say you feed the reader information without slowing the pace . . .

Coppel: I try to.

Yet your books do contain a great deal of information and realistic detail.

Coppel: It isn't there just for its own sake. Fact and detail give a work verisimilitude. Still, one must convey the information in an interesting way. This is easy for me because I am interested in it myself. For example, I write easily about machines and functions because they intrigue me. I am not one of those writers who is so aesthetically oriented that I can't put a nut on a bolt. I can, and I do. Well-made, functional machines please me. I love boats and airplanes and automobiles. There is a great deal of beauty in machinery.

How do you come by all this information?

Coppel: I'm an intellectual jackdaw. I collect bits and pieces. Not just about machines, of course. About everything. And necessary information is always available if one is willing to search it out. In THIRTY-FOUR EAST the pilot of the presidential airplane has to die in such a way as to cause the aircraft to crash quite unexpectedly. Now, pilots who fly presidents are closely watched by the medics. My pilot had to die of something that would not show up in a normal flight physical examination. So I went to an internist and said, "Look, this is my problem. How do I kill this character in the necessary way?" I had to learn the mechanisms of a particular death. Once I had those mechanisms, I could describe the onset of death realistically and write the scene as it needed to be written. In real time I was dealing with something that happens in thirty seconds or less. But I could stretch it out to the point where the suspense and the actual pain becomes so real to the reader that he feels it himself. I had to do it that way. I had to show the reader what was happening inside this dying man's chest, because a little rip in his aorta was about to shake the world.

Do you keep files?

Coppel: No. I write surrounded by scraps of paper. They aren't well organized, but just the act of writing things down as notes fixes them in my mind. When I'm finished, I clean house and get ready to start over again on the next project.

How much do you draw on your own experience?

Coppel: Some. Not much. I tend to extrapolate. In other words, I ask myself what I would do given the situation I postulate in my fiction. Autobiography is a stage writers must pass through, I suppose. I did it with NIGHT OF FIRE AND SNOW, which was heavily autobiographical. But autobiography has a tendency to degenerate into self-justification. I have outgrown that, I hope. Besides, fiction isn't life, and life sure as hell isn't fiction. Fiction demands order and plan. Life has neither: no beginning, middle or end, at least not in any sense that I can see. Fiction—the writer's interior life—has these elements of beginning, progressing and coming to a satisfactory ending.

Yet fiction must be lifelike surely?

Coppel: Of course. Life teaches the writer who then reorders what he has learned to create fiction.

Both A CERTAINTY OF LOVE and THE LANDLOCKED MAN are love stories, and both end tragically. Do you believe this must be so?

Coppel: Yes. The state of being in love is so demanding that no human being can maintain it indefinitely. Great love affairs either end tragically or just fizzle out—which is, in itself, a tragedy. In THE LANDLOCKED MAN I write about a love affair between a man of fifty and a girl in her early twenties. Such a love affair must of necessity be limited in its endurance. If you project it twenty years hence what do you have? A dodderer of seventy and a restless woman in her late thirties. My Martin and Christy are limited in the time they have to love one another, and this makes it touching and poignant. But everything changes, people most of all. Hell, we change from moment to moment. Constancy is not the greatest human attribute. Perhaps that's what makes life such a challenging business.

Many of your books are written in the first person. Why?

Coppel: I find the style easy. But, of course, some books require a multiple viewpoint and can't be done in the first person. Sometimes I have been able to combine first and third person, as in ORDER OF BATTLE. By writing of my protagonist in the first person and the other characters in third, I was able to show a group of men and women under the stress of war from the inside and out, as it were. For that book it worked. Others need a different approach.

Most writers encounter hang-ups and blocks from time to time. Do you? And what do you do about it?

Coppel: I run into my share of writing problems, and your question opens up something I think is really important. One of the facets of writing talent is the ability to sense when something is going bad, turning sour. This is terribly important, and yet there is no way to describe exactly what that mental process is. For me it is as though my mind is throwing up roadblocks, making the wrong way difficult to take. When this happens, I don't try to force the work. I go for a drive, or go sailing or fishing, anything to give me a different platform on which to stand while I consider my fictional world. It helps. Maybe it liberates the subconscious. A sail on the Bay or an afternoon standing in a trout stream unlocks the creative process. Much of THE LANDLOCKED MAN was "written" while fishing in Pescadero Creek.

Can you be specific about the sort of thing that slows you down or blocks you?

Coppel: Every novel is pinioned on certain critical points, and the narrative must move smoothly from one to the next. If this isn't happening easily, there is trouble ahead. But it is almost impossible to be more specific because writing is such a subjective enterprise. A bad day can be caused by anything from distractions to low blood sugar. I mean anything at all. The trick is to know when there are genuine difficulties that need thinking out and when you are simply being lazy. Basically, I'd say that if one knows where one is heading with a novel, the difficulties are few. And towards the end, they disappear entirely and the work goes almost of its own volition. Writers lead an interior life that is so real it tends to make them a bit schizophrenic. To me, my fictional characters are more real than actual people. At least this is so when a book is going well and nearing the end.

Do you always know exactly where your book is going? Do you plot that carefully?

Coppel: The answer to that is yes and no. Yes to where the novel is heading. If I haven't got that in hand, I don't really have a novel. And no to the question about careful plotting. I try to stay loose enough so that my fictional people and their story can develop along natural lines. It will, if I let it. But I don't try to keep my characters on a tight leash, forcing them to do things that are right for some predetermined plot but wrong for them. If you try to drive your fictional people, you only force them—and yourself—into dead ends. People, a general story line, and an ending. That's about all that's needed to begin a novel. Oh, yes, I like to have a title, too. It makes me feel secure, I guess. That's a bit childish, but there it is.

People, a story line and an ending. And your instinct?

Coppel: Yes, writer's instinct is what keeps the whole process working properly.

What about starting a book. Is that difficult?

Coppel: Damned difficult. For me, it is the most difficult part of the writing process. Beginnings are tough because you must capture your reader's attention and at the same time set the scene, introduce characters, lay out the situation. That is why I might think about a novel for months before sitting down to write. The beginning has to be right.

Once you have a beginning, does the rest go fast?

Coppel: Yes. I'm a fast-paced writer. Others I know are not. It has nothing to do with talent or even craftsmanship. I start at about nine in the morning and work until about two—or later, if it is going really well. And when I'm on the home stretch, there isn't any limit to the time I'll spend working each day. I go until I'm worn out and can't work any more. I get pretty raunchy at those times, and my friends know enough to leave me alone until I'm done.

Do you rewrite much?

Coppel: Very little. Almost not at all. I do have my wife read the day's output to me in the evening, and if there are bad patches I go back and redo them immediately. Incidentally, there are two schools of thought about hearing your prose read aloud. Some writers don't believe in it. I do. If what you have written can stand being read aloud, you know it works.

You have written under the names "Robert Gilman" and "A. C. Marin." Why the pseudonyms?

Coppel: For about four years running I was doing three books each year: a novel, a science fiction book and a thriller. My publisher didn't want three Coppel books on their list at the same time. Perhaps they felt the critics might think I was spreading myself too thin. They had a point, I suppose. When critics can't think of anything serious to carp about, they are capable of attacking a writer's working habits.

Do you regard your pseudononymous work less seriously than your Coppel books?

Coppel: Not for a moment. My thrillers and science fiction get the same best effort a novel gets. The only real difference is length.

How does "A. C. Marin" work?

Coppel: The same way Alfred Coppel does. There is the length difference, of course. Thrillers tend to be shorter and so can deal with less complex themes and still hold together well.

Which do you think is your best book?

Coppel: I don't write books of a single genre, so it is difficult to compare one with another. As a piece of novelistic craftsmanship, a work that is complex, well-conceived and properly paced, I'd have to give the nod to THIRTY-FOUR EAST. If what one looks for is sensitivity and intuitions about life, then I'd say THE LANDLOCKED MAN or A CERTAINTY OF LOVE are best. I think that the best chronicle, the clearest picture of a whole era of Americana I've done, is A LITTLE TIME FOR LAUGHTER. Whoever reads that book and can remember the Forties, Fifties and early Sixties should be able to say, "Damn—that's really the way it was in those days."

A LITTLE TIME FOR LAUGHTER *and* THE LANDLOCKED MAN *seem very personal, intimate books . . .*

Coppel: So they are. They are deeply introspective, and I think you could say that the attitudes expressed in them are pretty much what my attitudes are in my private dealings with those around me.

What do you have in progress now?

Coppel: A novel called THE BOYAR CONSPIRACY. It is an international adventure story, something like THIRTY-FOUR EAST in scope and pace. But different.

One last question. What makes a man become a novelist?

Coppel: A desire to create a special world—or many special worlds into which readers can escape. And then there is the freedom. It isn't a free life in the sense of being able to do as one pleases, because a novelist is one of the most compulsively driven men in the world. But there is the intellectual freedom. You can create any sort of reality you choose—and then you can live in it. It is as simple—or as complicated—as that.

NOVELS

Hero Driver. New York: Crown Publishers, 1954. (Pocket Books, 1955.)

Night of Fire and Snow. New York: Simon and Schuster, 1957. (Fawcett Crest, 1958.)

*__Dark December.__ Fawcett Gold Medal, 1960.

A Certainty of Love. New York: Harcourt, Brace & World, 1966. (Avon Books, 1968.)

Gate of Hell. New York: Harcourt, Brace & World, 1967. (Pinnacle Books, 1972.)

Order of Battle. New York: Harcourt, Brace & World, 1968. (Fawcett Crest, 1970.)

A Little Time for Laughter. New York: Harcourt, Brace & World, 1969. (Fawcett Crest, 1972.)

Between the Thunder and the Sun. New York: Harcourt Brace Jovanovich, 1971. (Pinnacle Books, 1972.)

The Landlocked Man. New York: Harcourt Brace Jovanovich, 1972.

Thirty-four East. New York: Harcourt Brace Jovanovich, 1974. (Popular Library, 1975.)

Under the pen-name of "A. C. Marin" Alfred Coppel has written the following thrillers:

The Clash of Distant Thunder. New York: Harcourt, Brace & World, 1968. (Pinnacle Books, 1971.)

Rise with the Wind. New York: Harcourt, Brace & World, 1969. (Pinnacle Books, 1972.)

A Storm of Spears. New York: Harcourt Brace Jovanovich, 1971. (Pinnacle Books, 1972.)

*Published only in paperback.

Under the pen-name of "Robert Gilman" Alfred Coppel has written the following science fiction books:

The Rebel of Rhada. New York: Harcourt, Brace & World, 1968. (Ace, 1970.)

The Navigator of Rhada. New York: Harcourt, Brace & World, 1969.

The Star Khan of Rhada. New York: Harcourt, Brace & World, 1970.

Ernest J. Gaines

Ernest Gaines lives on the second floor of a large apartment building at the corner of Golden Gate Avenue and Divisadero Street in San Francisco. About six feet tall, and stocky, he greets us dressed in a sweat suit and sneakers, a towel wrapped around his neck. We pass the small white writing table which stands against a wall between the two doors leading off the small square foyer. Beneath its legs yellow sheets of legal paper lie scattered like leaves.

In the living room a barbell lies on the wooden floor in front of a divan. There's a stereo across the room and hundreds of stacked records: Lightnin' Hopkins, Mississippi Fred McDowell, Gershwin, Schubert. He settles into a cushioned chair facing the overflowing brick and board bookcases beneath the windows. Behind him the glassed-in upper shelves of an old oak china cabinet hold more books, and the cupboards beneath are crammed with old manuscript pages, some handwritten, some typed.

We begin the interview, and at first, his answers seem stiff and uncomfortable as he sits with his arms lying flat on the armrests and his feet firmly planted on the floor. After a few minutes, however, he relaxes. He leans forward, then back. His hands begin to move, spreading apart, palms up, or pointing for emphasis. Though he speaks without a trace of a Southern accent, the South is present in him and in the room. He refers often to a number of framed black and white photographs taken during his yearly trips back to Louisiana. At the end of the interview he shows us each picture in turn, closer up: a huge old oak, "Miss Jane's oak"; a cyprus; a pecan tree stripped bare in winter; a portrait of a small boy in the dark cavern of a barn door; his aunt who "never walked a day in her life"; and finally, the buildings on the former plantation where he lived as a child—the plantation store, the white church, and the house, a wooden house with a sloping tin roof, where he was born. He is writing a new book called IN MY FATHER'S HOUSE which he has started many times before and which has, he says, "been kicking my ass around for ten years."

RH

When you start a book, where do you start? Do you have an idea, an event, an ending, a character?

Gaines: Well, I don't know. I have different ways to start different books. CATHERINE CARMIER, my first novel, took me so long to write that now I've forgotten how I started. I wanted to write about the place that I'd come from and the people I knew, so I made up a story about what I knew as a child.

OF LOVE AND DUST, my second novel, started with an idea. A white man can go with a black woman in Louisiana, but it's against all the rules for a black guy to go with a white woman, and I had known many different cases where this had happened, and certain little things reminded me of what I wanted to do. I was in a nightclub once where I saw a knife fight between two boys, two blacks, young men, and the fight was stopped before either of them got really hurt. Now, I also know an incident where a friend of mine got in a fight like that, and he killed a guy. Three guys jumped on him, and he killed one of them. He was sent to prison. He had been working for the white man, and this man could have gotten him out if he wanted to come out, but he said, "I'd rather spend my time because I killed this guy." So, he went to jail; he went to Angola, the state prison of Louisiana, and he spent five years.

Then, I listen to music. I play records all the time. I have a large collection of jazz, blues, and folk music. Lightnin' Hopkins, one of my favorite blues and folk singers, sings something about the worst thing that a black man ever done was moving his wife and family to Mr. Tim Moore's farm. Mr. Tim Moore's man, the overseer, would never stand and grin: "You keep out the jailhouse, nigger; I'll keep you out the pen."

When I started writing OF LOVE AND DUST, I thought of this boy who could have been taken out of that prison and put on this farm to work under a man like Lightnin' Hopkins was singing about. So, the Lightnin' Hopkins song reminds me of what could have happened to my friend. Of course, he would have been almost a slave to the man who had gotten him out, and he would have had to do everything the man said.

This is very chaotic, it doesn't make any sense, but when you ask how a novel begins in the mind, a little incident like this makes the novel. When I started writing the book, I had one guy kill another, and I had him bonded out of jail and put on a plantation to go through all the hell, but as soon as he could run, he runs. One incident led to another, and then it was up to the imagination. I suppose it's up to the writer to use his own experience, what he has heard, seen, tasted, touched, felt, and make a novel out of it.

In the case of THE AUTOBIOGRAPHY OF MISS JANE PITTMAN, I wanted to write a folk biography. At first, a group of people were going to tell about this one person's life, and through telling of this one person's life, they were going to cover a hundred years of history, superstitions, religion, philosophy, folk tales, lies—they were going to cover all this. After I'd written it like that one time, it was untrue, so I broke it down to one person telling the story, the individual herself telling the story, so instead of a short biography of Miss Jane Pittman it became THE AUTOBIOGRAPHY OF MISS JANE PITTMAN. I wanted to get it as a series of conversations, and what led me to that, I suppose, is that I grew up in the South around old people. My aunt—her picture's over there against the wall—was the lady who raised me. She never walked a day in her life, she was crippled all her life, and she raised us, me and my brothers and sisters. People used to come to our house because she couldn't go to their houses, and what they would talk about was something that I had thought about, that was worth writing about. But, of course, the actual writing was my imagination, what they had probably talked about, and more than they talked about because they couldn't know all the things I put in the book. These are the kinds of things that lead to novel or short story writing.

Is Miss Jane modeled after your aunt?

Gaines: Oh, no. Miss Jane walks all the time. My aunt never walked a day in her life. But, morally, her strength, her moral strength, yes, and my imagination and my conception. . . . You know, here's a black woman who is on her toes. Not all black women are like Miss Jane. In a few of the records there are a certain number of women who went through the things that Miss Jane did, but not all the things that she did. On the other hand, Miss Jane didn't go through as much as some others did. My imagination is limited.

MISS JANE *starts out very much as a physical odyssey—*

Gaines: Absolutely, it's supposed to be that way. I wanted several levels of literary form, several levels, with journeys, hard, physical things, and then it develops. In the beginning she's young, so it's her strength against nature. Then she goes on and becomes experienced. That's when she gets involved in other things like superstitions, and dreams, and the old voodoo woman. Then there's the symbolic thing of the horse, and the romantic thing of the beautiful octaroon with the son of the plantation owner which is a different level. Maybe I did not really go far enough, but these things are the things I was trying to aim at in her story because when people are telling stories they become realistic, naturalistic, fatalistic, romantic. . . . At the very end, Miss Jane becomes a different thing altogether. She becomes almost a recorder of history. When she talks about Jimmy and the quarters, she's not directly involved in anything that happens. Jimmy is The One. So, she's gone from action in the first part to just sitting down and observing things in the latter part of the book. There's several, I think, literary approaches running about in the book.

Do you think this shift in focus, on her at first and then opening out to include all Southern blacks, is a particular strength of the book? Did you do what you wanted to?

Gaines: Well, I feel I did what I wanted to do. I didn't do as much as I wanted to, but I had it completely under control. I knew what I was doing at all times. Maybe, I didn't do enough, but I knew what I was doing, and the only thing I would do if I wrote it over is do a little bit more, concentrate a little bit more.

On what specifically?

Gaines: Oh, really think more about the horse and the Joe Pittman thing, her travels, her conversion from sinner to religious person. I'd read much more on folklore, black folklore, on religion and the ministry, on the interpretation of religion. I would go further into the voodooism. I'd try to learn much, much, more about history. But I knew what I wanted to do. I wanted to start with an individual, with the problems that an individual confronts and then spread it out to the problems of the race. It didn't accidently happen.

The reason I ask all this is that Faulkner says that if you do your work right, your characters stand up on page 275, and all you have to do is take notes on what they do.

Gaines: Oh, yeah. I agree there, that lots of times Miss Jane would take over, but I had to have an idea. When I was writing this book, I did a lot of research. I did a lot of reading in history, by black as well as white historians. I read a lot of black folklore. I read a lot of interviews with ex-slaves, the WPA interviews with ex-slaves in the Thirties. By the time you get to page 275, if you've really developed the characters well and put them into action, they'll take over, but you have to deal with direction. You must invent some incidents along the way, and when Miss Jane gets into the incident, she'll develop it for you. I'm not saying that I knew when I was writing page 50 that I knew what I was going to say on page 60 or page 65, but I had an idea of which way I was going. I don't just sit down without any idea. A novel is like getting on a train to Louisiana. All you know at the moment is that you're getting on the train, and you're going to Louisiana. But you don't know what the conductor is going to look like; you don't know who you're going to sit behind, or in front of, or beside; you don't know what the weather is going to be when you pass through certain areas of the country; you don't know what's going to happen South; you don't know all these things, but you know you're going to Louisiana. You know you're going by train, and that it's going to take so many hours, days. . . .

Your dialog is remarkably true to the ear. It seems to us, as readers, to be exactly the way those people talk. We were wondering whether that came from memory. Did you have to spend a lot of time making your characters sound as they sound?

Gaines: Well, memory, work, a lot of work, and then I go back South all the time, I go South every year. I go for the Mardi Gras, and I stay two or three weeks. In 1963 I stayed six months. I go back all the time, and I had my grandmother, who just died a couple of years ago. She had never forgotten her Southern attitudes, or Southern ways, or Southern language. There are always relatives or friends going South, and most of the people here are first generation Californians, really transferred Southerners. And I read Southern writing. Faulkner was great at interpreting the Southern black dialog. He's as good at catching the Mississippi dialogue and putting it down on paper as anyone else I've read.

I really read my dialog. I check it out to see if it sounds exactly that way. And I've always been influenced by reading plays. I've always liked listening to the radio. I grew up on the radio, rather than television, and I used to spend hour after hour listening to the radio. So, you're listening to dialog, you're listening to dialog all the time, and you're hearing the good dialog as well as the bad. I remember when I was a child, *Gunsmoke* had probably the best dialog. I can still remember that. I could follow the story well just by listening. That's one of the reasons why in a lot of my books there's somebody listening through a wall to somebody talking. Somebody's always talking in another room. Maybe that's the radio.

In dialog writing you've got to listen, and you've got to read, and you've got to come to the point as quickly as you possibly can. Hemingway can use the word as well as anybody. When people talk, they always leave out words, they always understate things. Whether they are teachers, or farmers, or students, they always understate things.

If I just had to write dialog, I could write several pages a day, but I like to go over it. All the stuff you see back there on the floor is writing I did last week that I have to rewrite this week. I might write five pages one day, and then I might rewrite them the next day to perfect the sound, the dialog, as well as try to get the descriptions down.

Do you find it harder writing descriptions?

Gaines: Yes, I think everybody sees that in my writing. It's very hard for me to write descriptions. I like the sound of people's voices, and I think what a man says can very well tell what he's thinking, whether he's lying or not.

Just by the sound of his voice?

Gaines: Well, not by the sound, that's not exactly true, but I think you can develop a personality by listening to the sound of the voice. It says a lot of things. You can listen to the voice and tell, at least I try. . . . This is my best weapon, the dialog, and I try to do as much as I can with it. And I use the description when I cannot get away with the other thing. I'm not good at it, and I know it, and I have to work harder at description and straight narrative than dialog. Dialog is much simpler for me. My aim is to perfect it as much as I possibly can.

You said there were five pages on the floor from last week. How do you physically go about writing. Do you write every morning? Do you use a typewriter?

Gaines: No, I write longhand. That's the longhand stuff. I write longhand once, twice, or three times, and then I type two or three times, and then I consider that a draft.

Do you write every day?

Gaines: Oh, yes, I write every day. I get up to write.

Early in the morning?

Gaines: I try to write about nine, and work until about two. I stop for coffee, maybe eat a bowl of soup and some crackers. I try to get four hours in, five if it's going slow.

You said you re-write a lot. Do you feel that you have to get one thing right before you can go on to the next?

Gaines: Recently, I've been doing it because I'm getting older. When I first started writing, I would go through an entire book before I started writing one line over. And I don't know, now I'm a bit more conscious, and well, since critics are beginning to notice what I've been doing, I try to get things done well before I go someplace else.

Your last story in BLOODLINE *is told from multiple points of view. Is this just an experiment or were you really trying to work something out?*

Gaines: Oh, no, no, it's nothing original, because if you read Faulkner, you know Faulkner has done it and that other writers have done it. I wanted a different interpretation about this lady's life, how others in the community felt about her life, and I wanted them to tell it from their point of view.

Don Stanley, who used to review for the EXAMINER, said that BLOODLINE wasn't just a series of stories, but an episodic novel. You begin with a six-year-old child whose view is limited. He's this tall and can interpret so much of life, and the whole action takes place on this plantation. The eight-year-old boy in "The Sky is Gray" goes into a southern city where he discovers the race thing and white people. "Three Men" is a little broader. That is, because of Southern life, one black is taking the life of another, and he has to pay for it in the same way. Oh, BLOODLINE is something else. In each story, I use a different kind of stylistic approach. The last story is just a different way to look at the situation, I suppose. And, as I said before, I wanted people around to give their own personal views. And of course the sound of the language, I like the sound of individuality, and this is one of the things I've used. Different people tell it differently: the little boy, the guy from the city, the white woman, the old people. I want sounds, different sounds, different angles, as when you set up a camera.

In OF LOVE AND DUST, *the white overseer's children by Pauline, the black girl, are strong and healthy, while Tite, his child by Louise, his wife, is weak and ill. Is this symbolic?*

Gaines: Yeah, that's when you play with symbolism you hate later, the decadence of the West, the decadence of an idea. If Don Bon and Pauline had married, they would have had the most beautiful, productive and strong children, but he must stay with Louise. This is the kind of crap you hate later on, but at that time, I was pretty hungry.

How did you decide to have a detached narrator, Jim Kelly, tell the story in OF LOVE AND DUST *rather than Marcus, the hero?*

Gaines: When you get to Marcus, you get a one-sided thing. It's like trying to get Gatsby to tell the story of THE GREAT GATSBY. You can't do that. I needed a guy who could communicate with different people. I needed a guy who could communicate with Bon Bon, the white overseer, with Aunt Margaret, with Marcus. Marcus could never communicate with the people around him, and Jim could. I had to get a guy who could fit in like that. Fitzgerald used Nick because he could communicate both with Gatsby and with the real rich. Some of the younger blacks have criticized Jim as being an Uncle Tom, but I had to get a guy who could communicate with different sides, with the most conservative as well as the most radical and militant. And all through this, he must be able to learn to love, to try to understand. Even though he does not, he must try to. . . . Marcus said, "The hell with it, let the world burn; I don't give a damn."

Is the character of Marcus modeled after the friend you spoke of earlier who knifed a guy and went to jail?

Gaines: My friend did not come out of jail. Marcus comes out of jail. But if my friend had come out of jail, he might have been like Marcus. I wrote the story "Three Men" before I wrote OF LOVE AND DUST. In "Three Men" he stays in jail. I kept thinking of things, and eventually I went back to "Three Men". I said, "What would happen if my boy comes out of jail? What would he do?" And I said, "With this guy's attitude about things, he isn't going to give up five years of his life on this plantation to work and to pay for his bond if he finds a way of escaping." And my imagination began to race.

Marcus is a person who doesn't believe anything is going to happen to him. The rebel must have this: "Nothing in the world can ever happen to me. I'm not going to believe in anything else in the world but me and what I can do for myself." You see, Marcus was pre-revolutionary, pre-Civil Rights. Marcus looked after Number One. He was always Number One, and unless I have him thinking like that, I don't have a book. So, you play along a little. I know that doesn't answer, but that's the way it works in the book.

When you read another writer are you consciously aware of looking for things you might be able to use?

Gaines: Well, usually when I read, I read because I like to read. I love to read just like anybody else who loves literature. But I think I read carefully, and I see how a guy develops a scene. For example, I've hunted, but I like to see how it's done by other writers. Turgenev did it so well in A SPORTSMAN'S SKETCHES. Hemingway has done it. And Faulkner, you know, what he does with the smell of the trees when the weather is hot or when there's been a light rain, things like this. Every now and then I might read a woman writer to find out how a curtain should hang. I don't know these kind of things. You put a carpet on the floor that way; drapes should hang that way, two inches off the floor. I might read a woman writer or a man who can describe these things, and I would pay careful attention. Tolstoy did things with the eyes, you know, the batting of the eyelashes, which other writers could not do, so I look to see how Anna Karenina bats an eyelash, that kind of thing.

What writers have influenced you the most?

Gaines: Hemingway and Faulkner are my two heroes, I suppose, in American literature.

Why?

Gaines: Well, Hemingway has influenced every American writer since Hemingway, and Faulkner has influenced every Southern writer since Faulkner, and I'm a Southern writer, I suppose.

I admire Hemingway because of this grace under pressure thing which I think is more accurate of the black man in this country than the white man. Hemingway, without his knowing it, without a lot of the younger blacks realizing it, was writing as much about Joe Louis or Jackie Robinson as he was about any white man. The bull ring, the fight, the war, blacks do this sort of thing all the time, daily. Not all of them come out gracefully under pressure, but many of them do, especially those who accomplish anything.

It was Forster who said that Hemingway only wrote long short stories, that he didn't write a real novel because he was always finished in such a short period of time. He said there was not enough time for the characters to develop and this sort of thing. I would disagree because if enough pressure is put on a man, anything that can happen in the world can happen in twenty-four hours.

I've read a lot of Greek tragedies, so I know what it means to be confined to a day's space and time. When I wrote "A Long Day in November" I used certain rhythms, simple rhythms confined to a day. My life, my people's lives, have always been in limited spaces, limited areas, and there's always been a limited time of happiness, a limited time of this, a limited time of that, so my life can fit very appropriately in limited time, in limited area. I come from a plantation. Most of our activities were on this plantation, this road with houses on either side of it, the church there, the grocery store owned by the plantation owner at the front, and we worked in the fields, and most of the people I knew, their lives were confined to that area. Greek tragedy is confined, and it fits well with my experience because I was confined, my people have always been confined. And this is the kind of thing I do, although I've been criticized by, I think, Granville Hicks. He said Gaines always seems to round things off at the end. Ah well, what's the use of prolonging the goddamned stuff?

Has Ralph Ellison influenced you?

Gaines: No, I'm afraid he hasn't influenced me in any way.

Do you mind commenting on why?

Gaines: When I went to school, first at San Francisco State and then Stanford, the emphasis was on styles, on how to write truly, on how to write well. Most of your teachers knew that you had something to say, and they were trying to help you bring it out. But in all the creative writing classes I took there were no stories by black writers. You must realize, at the time, Ellison was not the big man he is today. In the mid-Fifties INVISIBLE MAN was out but nobody was assigning it, nobody was reading this book. You were just beginning to read Baldwin's essays, NOTES OF A NATIVE SON, you were just beginning to read these things. There was very little emphasis upon writing by black writers. So, since I could not write what the white writer was writing about, I could learn how to write technically from what the white writers were doing. The emphasis was on how to write. Many younger blacks are influenced by different concepts, the "black is beautiful" thing. Well, I knew that, you know, years ago when I first started writing. All I wanted to know was how to bring it out. These books weren't available in the Fifties so, of course, I didn't read them. By the time I read them, I knew what I wanted to do and the way I wanted to do it.

Do you ever get writer's blocks?

Gaines: Oh, yeah. The novel I'm working on now is a novel I tried to work years ago and never could. It defeated me every time I tried to work it, it just defeated me.

I spent five years writing my first book because I didn't know how to write a book, five years. My first book was published in '64. My second novel was published in '67, three years later, but it only took me eight months to write. Between '64 and '67 I was trying to write novels, but I just couldn't get another novel written. I wrote three or four books set in California, these unpublished things in here, different drafts of four or five books.

Would you say more about the problems of writing about California?

Gaines: I've been here now over twenty-four years; I've been here twenty-four years this month. I think it's the Southern thing in me that I just cannot—I must get it out whether it takes another two or three years or the rest of my life. I think I must really get that out of me before I can do the California thing. It's like Caldwell, who fell apart once he stopped writing about Georgia. Joyce would probably have fallen apart once he stopped writing about Dublin. Or Richard Wright, who did not write anything really great once he left the American scene. I doubt that Faulkner could have written anything great after he left Mississippi. I don't think THE FABLE is one of his greater books. So, maybe we're only made to write one book, I mean about one thing. Maybe that's why I haven't written a California thing. I think for the rest of my life I'll have something to write about Louisiana. I haven't touched the surface yet. I have so much to do.

NOVELS

Catherine Carmier. New York: Atheneum, 1964.

Of Love and Dust. New York: The Dial Press, 1967. (Bantam Books, 1969.)

The Autobiography of Miss Jane Pittman. New York: The Dial Press, 1971. (Bantam Books, 1972.)

SHORT STORIES

Bloodline. New York: The Dial Press, 1968. (Bantam Books, 1970.)

CHILDREN'S BOOKS

A Long Day in November. New York: The Dial Press, 1971.

Leonard Gardner

Leonard Gardner lives in the upper flat of a restored Victorian house in the Mission District of San Francisco. A thin six-footer, he greets us dressed in Levi cords, a sport shirt, and a V-neck sweater.

Upstairs, the rooms are neat, clean, and sparsely furnished. There are bookcases filled with works of fiction and non-fiction. There is also a volume of paintings by Edvard Munch, and in the bedroom two of Gardner's own paintings, a frontal nude and a portrait of his grandfather, both showing an expressionistic influence.

Back in the living room he sits in a round bottomed, curved back, wooden chair and talks about his work with a quiet intensity, his right arm describing an arc in the air. It's obvious he cares a great deal about boxing, boxers, and his craft. He is the author of what many consider to be the best book ever written about boxing.

RH

How did you become involved with the people you depict in FAT CITY?

Gardner: I got into the boxing scene in Stockton when I was eighteen. I'd been fascinated by boxing for some years before that because my father had been an amateur boxer and he was a great storyteller. I imagine my desire to write as well as my desire to box came from him, in part. Certainly the boxing did. I heard a lot about it when I was a kid. He gave me gloves and a punching bag, taught me a few things, and I boxed for years with all the kids in the neighborhood in the backyard. And at eighteen I went down to the gym where the fighters trained because by then I'd come to think of boxing as adventure, and I figured I had to get in on some of the real thing. So I started training seriously. I got acquainted with the boxers, and I really liked some of those guys. Some of them were farm workers. They weren't big time fighters. They weren't making any money to speak of, but to me they had an aura. And for years after that I carried that atmosphere, a feeling for those guys and the kind of life they were living.

What fascinates you about boxing?

Gardner: There's something about the struggle that fascinates me, of course, as it's fascinated many fiction writers. It's a very dramatic sport, beyond the spectacle. It's very much a test of will, what they call heart—how much self-belief there is, how much commitment, how much tenacity. A boxer is fighting his own self-defeat as much as he is his opponent. The fight fans get this vicariously, of course. They see this drama, and it's a catharsis for them. You can see this struggle in boxing whereas in the rest of us it's going on at a psychological level, mostly hidden.

The people in FAT CITY certainly seem to be losing. Do you consider yourself a grim or pessimistic writer?

Gardner: I really don't. I guess I have a strange way of looking at things. I re-read it not long ago, and it seemed grimmer to me then, after several years. But I found some humor there. The dialog never struck me as grim. There's something a little whacky about it. It seemed to me that I was writing about a kind of life lots of people live. I was writing about people I felt something for. If their story is grim, well, grimness is just part of life, certainly the life of a boxer or a farm laborer.

I read recently that the short-handled hoe which you describe in FAT CITY has been banned by the State of California.

Gardner: I was very happy to see that. When I was writing that chapter I hoped to bring to public attention the tortuousness of working with the short-handled hoe. It's notoriously hated work among farm laborers, and it's responsible for plenty of back trouble. I did a little farm work once, and I tried that, and I couldn't understand how men could go on for weeks and months working with that hoe. I met a man who said he'd worked with it for twenty-five years and never had got used to it. He was reeking of Sloan's Liniment, and his walk was almost like a duck waddle. Naturally, out there I got to thinking of how we all live off these people, and we don't know anything about them, and don't care. Getting through a day with that hoe is like getting through a bad lifetime.

Do you think a sense of justice plays a dominant role in a writer's concepts? It's apparent in FAT CITY.

Gardner: Yes, I think it does, and I think my sense of justice is obvious in FAT CITY. As you mention it, I remember how that's the main element of the book, really. Yet at the same time that I felt that people I'd known and observed like those in the book were being victimized by their culture, I felt they were people with some kind of class, dignity, color, drama and courage. And even the comic things, like absurd drunken scenes, seemed noteworthy, meaning they should be noted down and told to somebody. There are all kinds of injustice, including the injustice of fate and biology that we're unable to change. There's always going to be death, weakness, failure and loss, and lack of understanding. In the face of things of that nature, the courage and dignity of the individual would be a partial redemption. There's a kind of secret justice there within the confines of injustice that you can discern in literature, anyway. I think writing that comes from the heart gets at this. In other words the kind of writing that comes not from abstract concepts, such as justice, even, but from a writer's feelings, which include a sense of justice.

There is a lot of irony in FAT CITY. *Did you consciously strive for it?*

Gardner: I knew what I was after. I wanted irony, and it seems a natural part of the way I look at things. Besides it's hard not to be ironic when you're writing about something like boxing. The whole thing about a fighter that allows him to continue is confidence. There's a lot of self-delusion that seems necessary. If you're not optimistic, what the hell are you going to do in something like boxing? So anyway I saw that big gap between what actually was happening and what my characters thought their chances were.

Where did the title come from?

Gardner: I was in a museum looking at a show of photographs with a friend. In one picture some ironist had chalked FAT CITY on the side of a slum building. My friend said, "There's your title," and I felt it was.

In addition to the novel you wrote the screenplay for the movie. Were there any difficulties translating your book onto film?

Gardner: It was a lot of work, but it wasn't actually all that difficult to adapt because the book had a lot of scenes. I tried as much as I could to stick right with the novel. Naturally there are problems transposing narrative material to dramatic form, and there were diplomatic problems. I signed on determined that I'd do my damnedest to get what I'd written in the book onto the screen, that I wasn't going to let anything get in there that violated the sense of the story. So I imagine my situation was different from that of a professional screenwriter because I must have argued more. I imagine a professional screenwriter who wants to keep his job would be philosophical about changing things if the producer and director said, "We don't like it this way." I wasn't that malleable.

Obviously some changes were made since the book and the movie end differently. Do you think you succeeded in protecting your book?

Gardner: I suppose I did. One of the problems of doing a screenplay is that you're not alone. You're not the boss. A screenplay is a collaboration whether you want it to be or not because you don't have final say on what stays and what goes and what gets changed by somebody else. I wrote six or seven drafts of that screenplay, and the producers and the director always wanted me to get Tully and Ernie together in a scene at the end. I felt that the essential story would already be over by then, and so I resisted for awhile. But I could understand their feeling cinematically, and finally I got an idea I liked for a new final scene, and I agreed to make the change. I'd felt there wasn't any more for Tully and Ernie to say to one another by then, because Tully has met his built-in defeat. Loss has become a part of his identity, and all he wants is a little company. So I got the idea for that long final silence when they have that cup of coffee together and Tully begs Ernie to stay and talk. The scene becomes a kind of representation of Tully's spirit. He's come to the brink of life's emptiness. There *is* nothing to say.

Did FAT CITY *take a long time to write?*

Gardner: It was slow. I worked on and off for about five years on the book. At first I didn't clearly know what my plot was going to be. I thought it was mostly going to be about the kid, Ernie, but I saw when I had barely gotten into the novel that Ernie wasn't adequate for what I felt I wanted. I didn't think an eighteen-year-old knew enough about life or that his problems were universal enough.

Is the book autobiographical? Are you Ernie?

Gardner: No. He's a fictional character, although some of the things that happen to him happened to me. We got our noses broken under the same circumstances. The last chapter where he's put out of the car in the desert is a true story. And I worked in a skid row gas station and trained in that gym.

Did you have any idea where the book was going when you began, or was there only this feeling you've mentioned?

Gardner: It started with a feeling, an emotional perception of what was going on in skid row, and in boxing, what I saw happening there, and of who those guys were. I was trying to transfer this atmosphere, and the way you get atmosphere across depends a great deal on rhythm as well as the actual subject matter.

What do you mean by "rhythm"?

Gardner: It's cadence, the cadence of sentences and paragraphs.

Is there a rhythm to the book as a whole?

Gardner: I hope so. I had a definite design in mind. I had a sense of a circle—of closing the circle at the end. I guess that's a pretty limited view of form, but I think I did it.

Does the idea of a circle have any special meaning to you?

Gardner: Completeness, I guess. It's a terrific gratification to be able to round out something, make a meaning of something, get hold of the material enough to shape something satisfying. Since your own life is a process that never seems conclusive, that can seem inaccurate to your own character, there's a nice feeling when you're writing and things are working out all right

Do you think that personal experience is important in writing?

Gardner: Yes. You have to know the details of what you're writing about, but you also have to have faith that your experience is greater than you think it is. Imagination is a great assembler of pieces. You actually rely on it, and it relies on both your conscious and unconscious experience—and when you get into unconscious experience then you're getting into the mystery and excitement of writing. A character can be utterly unlike you, yet you're contradictory enough, complex enough, so that even though he's completely imaginary, you can be taking a facet of yourself that perhaps you hadn't even previously discovered or explored and put that into him, and maybe build his identity around it, so that you come to know what he'll do in certain situations.

Did you have a problem with the characters of FAT CITY running away with you?

Gardner: No, I don't think so. I wrote chapters that didn't belong, and some of those were about characters other than those in the finished book. What I did was take out whatever didn't contribute or wasn't very good. It was a matter of tightening up and leaving what seemed to be the heart of the subject.

Do you think writers are different from other people?

Gardner: I always assumed that they weren't. I think if you thought you were, your writing wouldn't have any depth. If you don't believe that what you feel is what other people feel, then how can you presume to create characters that are going to have any meaning to anybody else?

I noticed that your dialog in FAT CITY seems to express in a comic way how people seem to talk to each other as if they're not quite listening to each other and sometimes at cross purposes. Is dialog difficult for you to write?

Gardner: No. I've never had trouble with dialog. The narrative passages gave me much more trouble. I find that I often talk out loud when I'm writing dialog—to test it.

Who are the writers from whom you derived inspiration for your own writing? Who influenced you?

Gardner: I learned from a lot of writers: Hemingway, Faulkner, Conrad, Turgenev, Chekhov, Flaubert, Dostoevsky, Celine, Svevo. Those are writers that meant a lot to me. I think I got hope anytime I read anything great by a great writer.

What do you mean by "hope"?

Gardner: Inspiration. "They" made me love fiction. And that love gave me the desire to dedicate myself to writing fiction. And the dedication that I felt gave me the hope that I could do it.

What is the most difficult thing in writing for you?

Gardner: When I was working on FAT CITY I had a motto over my desk, and that was: THE ART OF THE NOVEL IS GETTING THE WHOLE THING WRITTEN. That's the most difficult thing.

NOVELS

Fat City. New York: Farrar, Straus and Giroux, 1969. (Dell, 1970.)

Herbert Gold

Herbert Gold works in a small apartment on the East side of Russian Hill in San Francisco. He is not large, around five-feet-seven and of medium build, but he seems more imposing, perhaps because of his black beard which is flecked here and there with silver. Dressed in a blue chambray shirt, old corduroys, and hiking boots, he leads us down a long, narrow hall. Posters of all kinds, including a reproduction of a painting by Bruegel, are tacked up along the walls. There is also a child's stick-figure drawing which proclaims, "I love my Daddy," in hand-printed letters. A small, windowless alcove off one side of the hall contains sagging bookshelves, an old door supported by concrete bricks which serves as a desk, a typewriter, and a free-standing card table piled high with paper and manila envelopes.

The end of the hall opens out into a small living room which has a couch, table, rocking chair, and a sweeping view of the San Francisco skyline from the Bay Bridge to the new Sutro Tower. Our host brings coffee, leans back in the rocking chair, and asks us what we're up to. Once satisfied, he answers all questions without hesitation in a rapid, articulate voice, gesturing occasionally with an open hand. He also volunteers information concerning others we might interview and agents or publishers who might help us.

When the interview is over, we return back down the hall to Gold's alcove working area and discover the funeral pictures he has brought back from a recent trip to Israel. A crippled father who lost both his legs in the first Arab-Israeli war sits in his wheel chair beside the graves of two of his sons killed in the latest conflict. Though Gold has seen them before, he waits patiently while we leaf through the photographs one by one. He shakes his head. "It's horrible," he says. "Horrible. . . ."

RH

How do you begin a book?

Gold: Books really begin in images and characters and, maybe, some kind of action. And someplace—I can't tell you where exactly—the theme or a sense of the action begins to come clear. It's clearest after I finish the first draft when I go back to tidy it up. I might insert new things in the first chapter because I discovered where I'd come out, and I wanted to have arrows leading to that door. Nabokov said something about this in his book about Gogol. He said Gogol was always careful to construct secure foundations for his work after he finished. I'm a very untidy writer in that—not beginning with a strict outline or sense of structure—I have to do it all afterwards. I just read Ann Charters' fascinating book about Kerouac. I don't believe in automatic writing because I want to be conscious of what I'm doing, but I like the speed and energy of automatic writing. So, if there's a semi-automatic writing, that's what I do. I try to get in touch with my fantasy life and my dream life by writing fast and stimulating myself. I get an almost metabolic speeding when it's really good. Things come out that startle me. They're coming out of my fingers, not out of my head. The difference between me and the writers who really live by automatic writing—someone like Kerouac—is I go back afterwards and question what I've said and cut and rewrite and change and rearrange. I take the lid off and let it boil out, but then I put the lid back on and sweep up.

How long does the sweeping up take?

Gold: Usually not very long. Once I've finished, I have a sense of where I'm going and what I intend, and the rewriting comes fast. And it's pleasurable because all the insecurity is gone. I know I've got something if I'm bothering to rewrite it. I've written manuscripts I've never published because I found the task of making something of them hopeless.

But intuition is important even though some manuscripts are hopeless?

Gold: Yeah, especially someone like me, because otherwise I wouldn't do anything. I have a lot of academic training, and, if I start to think, I write an essay. And I do write essays, and those are filled with thoughts outlined in advance.

Do you have any theory of creativity, what causes it, or why it works?

Gold: What makes the artist different from other people? I think it's partly metabolic. He has a rage to control a dream, give it direction, make it objective. There's a popular theory that the artist expresses his disability. He's wounded, he's the man with the gangrenous foot, the one with a psychological disability. He's impossible. He's weak; therefore he expresses. This applies to some, but there's the opposite: people with more than usual power, people with an overflow of power which requires that they get very rich, or conquer the world, or make poems. There's a little poem of Goethe's that says something like: "If God had wanted to make me a worm, he would have made me a worm, but in his great mercy, he made me Goethe." There's a kind of arrogance. The creative person says, "My vision is more valuable than other people's, and I think they better have it." Then he insists on giving it to you.

Do you remember the first time you wanted to be a writer?

Gold: I was standing at a water fountain. I had written a little theme, and my sixth grade teacher patted my head. Her name was Ruth Collins. I had written a sad story about a rattlesnake. She patted me on the head and said it was a good story, but that I had misspelled gruesome, which I spelled g-r-e-w, instead of the way it should be. But she smiled. This was the life for me.

Did you consciously set out to become a writer after that incident?

Gold: No. I had ideas about different things I wanted to be. I think the longest-lasting vocation I had in mind was "Philosopher." I went through school with the idea I could teach philosophy and write philosophy and be a philosopher. I never thought of being a professional writer until it happened that I was. And that I found by accident.

How did it happen?

Gold: Well, during the war I wrote poetry and published poetry. Then I wrote stories, and I won a contest in college. Somebody suggested I send a story to a magazine. The first commercial magazine that published me was HARPER'S BAZAAR, of all things. At the time they published so-called serious fiction. I was still in college and got the idea I was going to write for publication. After that, I didn't publish another story for a couple of years. My next story was in a tri-lingual magazine published in Rome called BOTEGHE OSCURO. But I didn't think of being a professional writer because I had a wife and two children very early. I didn't think I'd make a living at it. So, I went on doing other things to make a living. I taught, I edited an entertainment magazine, I worked as a hotel clerk, I scavenged all kinds of ways to make a living. I only discovered I could be a full-time writer without other jobs when I reached my thirties.

You've written twelve books, plus essays and short stories. You've also taught. Physically, how do you do so much?

Gold: I like doing it. That's the reason I do it. If I didn't, it would be torture. I'm not a hard-working person. Usually I'm through by noon. I have this place which is where I used to live before I remarried. I come here in the morning and write if I feel like it. Then I go about the rest of my business. If you write only a hundred words a day, you've written a lot by the end of the year. I don't write by word count, but, if you write a few sentences, and it's got a good direction, you're going to finish a book before long. Before I was married, when I lived here, I used to write sometimes before breakfast. I'd get up without washing my face and go to the typewriter, and it would just come out. A lot of FATHERS was written that way. It worked because I was dealing with my own dreams and fantasies and recollections. I found myself giving orders the night before. I'd have a problem with the book, so I told myself to dream it. And I'd wake up and go to the typewriter and write it. In some ways it was very easy to finish the book that, by that time, I'd spent more than fifteen years working on. The last chapters came very easily.

Some writers have described writing as agony, and yet you. . . .

Gold: Well, they've left out part of the story. When they say, "Writing is agony," they should add, "and I'm a masochist." If they add, "I enjoy my agony," then it's a fair statement.

How long does it take you to finish a book?

Gold: It varies a lot. I wrote THE PROSPECT BEFORE US from beginning to end in less than two months: fifty-eight days, which is actually a long time when you consider Balzac's speed. FATHERS I wrote over a period of seventeen years. THE OPTIMIST I never did finish. I'm not happy with it at all. I published it too soon. I think I had the germ of a good book, but I was personally distraught at the time. The book was somewhat a reflection of my personal feelings, so I didn't have good control of it. I wrote MY LAST TWO THOUSAND YEARS in a couple of years, but I'd done pieces of it sooner.

So you have more than one thing going at a time?

Gold: Yes, I don't like to strain. I think it gives hemorrhoids. So, if something isn't going well, I quit. I often write more than one book at a time, and I often interrupt a book to write a story or an essay. I was writing a book that was almost done, except for the last chapter, when I started another thing. That turned into MY LAST TWO THOUSAND YEARS, and I've abandoned the one that was almost done. For a long time I had the manila folders on a card table. I recently moved them into a drawer which is a sign of their going into exile for a long time.

What makes you decide not to finish something?

Gold: If it doesn't feel right. I could show you manila folders and boxes filled with several unfinished novels. Maybe they will be finished someday, but usually what happens after they sit awhile is that they either get ripe or they get rotten. In some cases they've gotten ripe, and in some cases I've just abandoned them. If it doesn't feel like it's developing, then I let it go. You do a little trick with yourself. You say, "Well, I'm putting it aside."

You mentioned to us once that you wrote a novel about a Haitian painter which made you think of Joyce Cary's THE HORSE'S MOUTH. You felt your book wasn't as good, so you dropped it. We were wondering if writers consciously try to stake out new territory to free themselves of comparisons which could be intimidating?

Gold: I think most writers are sure they're writing a masterpiece, and that conviction seems necessary to the work. I may, when I finish, decide such isn't the case, but, while I'm writing, it seems absolutely essential: The world requires this book. If the thought crosses my mind, as it did in the writing of that book, that it really parallels THE HORSE'S MOUTH, that it's not cutting out new ground except for this interesting exotic locale, then my intensity of feeling, my love of the book, vanishes. When I love a book no longer, I can't finish it.

Do you ever have moments when you feel you have nothing to say?

Gold: I get discouraged if I haven't anything to write or say, and it happens now and then. What I do is ignore it. I go on a trip or do a lot of walking or do a lot of exercising. I've found from so many years that it always comes back, so I can wait for it. Usually, it doesn't take too long. I think if you press, if you work at it, then you produce the blocks you're talking about. I've always been able to say to myself, "Well, I don't have to write. Nobody's asking me to write. I can make a living without writing now." So, if I'm not writing, why torture myself? Am I writing for my tombstone? No, I'm not.

Do you work at a typewriter?

Gold: Anyway that's convenient: pencil, pen, typewriter, on the back of menus, outside, inside, on napkins. The one thing I don't use is an electric typewriter, because it's too great an encouragement. I like the physical effort, the sculpturing.

As a writer, do you have any superstitions?

Gold: No, I have no superstitions. It's just that before I begin to write I pray on an altar with a cat's tail.

Have there been any particular writers who have influenced you?

Gold: The whole tradition of using American speech, from Mark Twain to early Saul Bellow, has influenced me. My father's broken English, and some of Dostoevsky's concerns have influenced me. Even a relatively minor writer, although a good one, Moravia, wrote one story which shook me and is imbedded in my brain.

Which one?

Gold: "Bitter Honeymoon." A French writer, Raymond Queneau, I should add to the list that includes Twain and Bellow and, maybe, Algren. I was learning French at the time I was reading Queneau. The way he used street French elegantly and stylishly was a clue to what I could do in English. On the purely surface level of style, Queneau influenced me maybe more than anyone else.

How would you characterize your style?

Gold: I'd say it was partly a voice; in other words, it could be read aloud. It's a verbal style, but cleaned up. I'm more garrulous in person than I am when I'm writing.

Are you very conscious of style when you're writing or revising?

Gold: I'm very conscious when I'm revising. In the first draft I get carried away by stylistic joys. It grieves me to cut out a good phrase that doesn't fit. I have frequent griefs of this sort. I think one of my faults as a writer is that if something in a funny story makes me laugh, even if it doesn't quite fit, I'll leave it in anyway. In fact, somebody said he showed Evan Connell a new story of mine a few months ago, and Evan said it was too clever. He's probably right. It's hard for me to make it unclever. I'm aware of my own voice, and I enjoy it, but what I really like most is the story coming out in me. Part of the cult of personality now is that style has become a character in the story, particularly in the new journalists like Tom Wolfe. Tom Wolfe is an important person in almost anything he writes. I think that is a flaw. Certain writers, Mailer is one, have been so fascinated by looking behind them to see what's coming out, that you tend to lose sight of what he's saying. At least I do, and I think his manner has gotten in the way of his talent.

How do you feel about the power you have in doing journalism?

Gold: There's a high in doing journalism because you do have this power to manipulate reality. The justification is that you decide that you're honest, smart, funny, perceptive, sympathetic, warm, nasty, brutish, and short, and, therefore, your vision is going to be the correct one. But certainly you can turn into a Rex Reed, and the only defense the public has is your own conscience. And since a lot of people are without conscience, it's a tremendous weapon. I like to deal with the real world, so I think information is important. The journalism I do helps to keep me in touch with what's going on.

How do you feel about "now" fiction?

Gold: I've written things that were reflections simply of a mood of a year. I wrote a whole series about disc jockeys. Most of them were published in PLAYBOY during its early years, and I know those are froth. But I may have some sense about commerce in America as a result of writing them. Mostly, I don't think about whether a thing is "now" or modern or historical or classical; I think about what it would be like doing it. If I like writing it, then it's worth doing. I worry about whether it's deep after it's done.

You mentioned once that you didn't publish your poetry. Why?

Gold: I tell my wife where it is, so someday, if anyone wants it, he can have it. But there's a definite reason for my not publishing it. I can write it without any sense of shaping it for an audience, without any suspicion of doing it to be pleasing or. . . . It's almost like writing a diary.

How much of that desire for acceptance enters your work, the desire to shape something for an audience?

Gold: That's a difficult question because I'm definitely writing for somebody. Writing is a form of communication, and I like an audience. Today I received galleys in the mail for a little story that's to be published in THE OHIO REVIEW, a quarterly published by Ohio University. I was out there as "writer in residue," and they asked me for a story, so I gave them a story and was glad to do it. But I would much prefer that a story of mine would be in a large circulation magazine. I believe, I guess, in a jury system rather than the judicial system. I'd rather be read by a hundred thousand good jurors than six good judges. I don't believe in the Supreme Court.

Speaking of the Supreme Court, how do you react when you get a bad review?

Gold: I react, probably, not well. I went through a period when I didn't care. Now I care. A reversion to second childhood. If it's a bad review by an idiot in an unimportant place, I shrug it off. If it's a bad review in an important medium, then I'm worried. I feel sorry for my publisher; I feel sorry for my agent; I feel sorry for myself. I feel sorry for my old mother and father who will have to read it. Once I had a bad review in NEWSWEEK by a writer who later apologized and told me he was trying to make his reputation by reviewing me that way. Someone told me recently that TIME's reviews are done in a day and a half from the time they get the book to the time the review is in print. You can't take a review like that very seriously. But what you do take seriously is that it's your livelihood, it's the way your cousins look at you.

Do you get any response to your work from the man in the street?

Gold: Americans are a very flighty people. If a book comes out and is a great success, I get a lot of letters, telephone calls, and then it passes. I'm not a celebrity and my face is not recognizable. When FATHERS was published, in one week my picture was on the front page of THE NEW YORK TIMES BOOK REVIEW, in TIME, NEWSWEEK, THE SATURDAY REVIEW, local newspapers, and some other places. I took a plane to New York and was recognized by the stewardesses. I was given great attention; I was recognized at the airport; I was an instant celebrity. I came back two *weeks* later and none of that. It was all over. Several new issues of TIME had come out. Several issues of NEWSWEEK had come and gone. There were new celebrities.

Do you consider yourself an optimist?

Gold: Metabolically. That is, I tend to be enthusiastic and enjoy experience, but what my metabolism tells me is true, my brain tells me is not true. I enjoy the beginning of a day, but I can see that history is not a happy place. The perfect thing would be to have both elements present in the same book. It's hard to do, and I'm trying to do it.

Which writers have done it?

Gold: Tolstoy at his best, Homer, Shakespeare, and, in a funny way, Nabokov. He's done it at different levels and very much through style and content. He's a very strong influence on a lot of writers now, Updike, for example.

Is there a central motivating philosophy in your work?

Gold: There are central concerns. I'd hate to have to name them, though I think I know what they are. I wrote an essay called "The Novelist's Life, and The Life Contained in Novels." It says a lot of what I think my work is about. It's in a collection called THE MAGIC WILL.

In SALT, Peter juggles oranges, which seems to be a central metaphor in the book. Do you consciously search for metaphors or symbols, or do they just happen?

Gold: I try to avoid symbols. The book began as a story, which is often what happens to me. I start writing a story, and it becomes a book. I wanted to write a book about a masturbater, and I thought of a stockbroker and his abstract manipulation of money. I truly don't remember how I got the idea of the juggler, but it became part of Peter's character.

Why do you normally try to avoid symbols?

Gold: Because that is not what fiction is about. Story is about story, not about ideas or symbols. If a symbol works, it's because it's not noticed as a symbol; it's noticed as an element in character or story. In THE PROSPECT BEFORE US, I discovered at the end of the book that I'd written a contemporary version of the Samson story. In the first draft of that novel, the hero's name was Sam Bowers, and I changed it to Harry because I didn't want the symbol to be noticed.

Why not?

Gold: Because people start thinking about structure and symbols rather than story.

Would you say a good symbol is accidental then?

Gold: No, it's the opposite of accidental: it's inevitable, therefore, it doesn't have to be planned.

So you believe a story or novel should not be too obvious as to its meaning or intention by the author?

Gold: It depends. I don't think the meaning should be obvious, if you mean message or symbol. I think it should be as clear as possible, if you mean action, the sense of character. The moral essence or symbolic value should exist on the unconscious level, so the reader knows, but doesn't know he knows. Take that famous line from a poem of Auden's which I think he later cut out: "We must love one another or die." That should be implicit, it shouldn't be explicit. Auden had the good sense to cut the line out of the revision, but it's still the meaning of the poem, insofar as the poem "means."

Do you have an idea how a story should end?

Gold: I have an image which I've lived with so many years it's part of my head. The end is like a child's slide. At the end is a little hook where it sails off again before the fall into the sand. You go down the slide and then up and away. There's that trajectory. At the end, life isn't over: the story goes on, but the rest of it goes on in your imagination. If it really ends, then it's dead.

Do you consider yourself a natural writer?

Gold: Yes, I do. That doesn't mean I'm good or bad, but I think I'm natural. I can't help telling stories. In fact, most of my critics would say I tell too many stories. And a lot of people have called me a natural liar. But I really get too much fun out of writing to stop. Actually, it would help me, probably, to write a little less, because people get tired of reading me, I think.

What are you working on now?

Gold: I just finished a draft of a book. Most of it came the way I like books to come. But one chapter was the most painful writing I've ever done. I struggled and struggled over it. And the struggle was not to write it, but to write it down. There's a difference. I went for a walk one night. I was thinking about what was happening, and the whole chapter came to me. The words were all in my head. All I had to do was write them. It took me two weeks. I would write a couple of sentences, and I would be exhausted. I couldn't do anything for the rest of the day. I was disgusted; I was revolted; I hated it. The only way I finally finished that chapter was to say to myself, well, I can just cut it out, I can destroy it, but I've got to write it down to see what I've got. Somehow—this never happened to me before—it went counter to my sensibility, to my sensibility or to my judgment, so powerfully that it really caused an anger against myself, in myself. And I haven't reread it: it's being typed. It may be very good, and it may be as bad as I felt it was. That was a new—here I am, forty-nine—that was a totally new experience for me. I cut. I hit something in myself. I hit something in myself that I found deeply disturbing. I carried it through, but I don't know what I've got. . . .

NOVELS

Birth of a Hero. New York: The Viking Press, 1951.

The Prospect Before Us. New York: World Publishing Company, 1954. (Award Books, 1964.)

The Man Who Was Not With It. Boston: Little, Brown and Company, 1956. (Random House, 1956; Avon Books, 1969.)

The Optimist. Boston: Little, Brown and Company, 1959. (Pocket Cardinal, 1965.)

Therefore Be Bold. New York: The Dial Press, 1960. (Lancer Books, 1961.)

Salt New York: Random House, 1963. (Pocket Books, 1964; Avon Books, 1971.)

Fathers. New York: Random House, 1966. (Fawcett Crest, 1966.)

The Great American Jackpot. New York: Random House, 1969. (Aco Books, 1970.)

Swiftie the Magician. New York: McGraw-Hill, 1974.

SHORT STORIES

Fifteen By Three. New York: New Directions, 1957. [Short stories by R. V. Cassill, Herbert Gold and James B. Hall.]

Love and Like. New York: The Dial Press, 1960.

NON-FICTION

The Age of Happy Problems. New York: The Dial Press, 1963.

*****Biafra Goodbye.** Two Windows Press, 1970.

The Magic Will. New York: Random House, 1971.

AUTOBIOGRAPHY

My Last Two Thousand Years. New York: Random House, 1972.

CHILDREN'S BOOKS

The Young Prince and the Magic Cone. New York: Doubleday & Company, 1973. [Illustrated by Julie Brinckloe.]

*No hardback edition of this book was published.

James Leigh

During the Spring of 1972 Jim, his wife Ria and their son Gabriel lived in a large rented house in the Sausalito hills with a magnificent view of San Francisco and the Bay. They had returned from their home in Spain when Jim accepted a teaching post for a year at San Francisco State University.

Jim is tall and easy-going. He obviously enjoys people and likes to entertain. The Leighs served lunch to us, after which Jim, Roger and I settled into the living room. Jim lit a Spanish cigarette, "One of my few luxuries," he told us, and we turned on the tape recorder.

He speaks easily with a writer's verbal facility with language and ideas and responded to our questions at length and without reserve.

We caught Jim during a time of transition when he was re-evaluating his past work and thinking forward to what he wanted to do next. Much of the interview reflects his broodings. . . .

DT

When did you first come to the Bay Area?

Leigh: In 1950. But I came to stay in '52. I was twenty-two. I wanted to become a jazz musician, and I thought San Francisco was the place to come. It's the only place I've ever lived that when people say "Where are you from?" it's a pleasure to tell them. There's a San Francisco snobbery—it can be incredibly backwater and bush league—that rubbed off on me. Also, the place where good things happen to you, you call your home. A lot of good things happened to me right here.

I grew up in Southern California, half a dozen different towns. I hadn't been to college, and I had this musician fantasy, having been a really heavy jazz head since I was about thirteen. I ran into some friends almost as hopeless on their instruments as I was to start with, and we got a little of that experience, beer bars in Santa Monica and Venice. We played one place, Georgia's Playroom, "Santa Monica's No. 1 Fun Spot," the sign said. A buck a head and all the draft Lucky Lager we could drink.

Why did you wait until you were twenty-two?

Leigh: Well, my father died when I was fairly young, and my mother went to work until I finished high school; then I got a job on a newspaper, THE SANTA MONICA EVENING OUTLOOK, and took care of my mother and little sister for five years. It was a very good thing for me. I was the head of the family, but without a lot of the pressures. Then my mother went back to work at Douglas Aircraft so I could take off.

Do you think you learned anything from being a newspaper man, or do you think that type of writing is destructive?

Leigh: Seeing my name daily in print in my own home town was a substitute for things I'd rather have been good at, say sex and sports. And the writing itself—well it was a *kind* of writing that allowed distinctions, better or worse. It may have addicted me to the ideal of making a living at the typewriter. I think it might have been destructive if I hadn't later run into a marvelous lady professor at San Jose State, an absolute perfectionist, who corrected my idea of myself as a polished writer of English prose. It took her ten weeks, and I almost flunked my other subjects. Dr. Josephine Chandler. I want that name down.

When did you first get interested in writing? Was it something you fell back on after the jazz?

Leigh: Not really. I was always interested in writing, always pretty good at it, and always got encouragement, first at home and then at school. When I was working on the paper, seventeen to twenty-one, it filled my life at first, that and trying to get laid. Then, when I was about nineteen I got re-interested in music. That got very important for the next few years, until after I moved up here to San Francisco, and a friend of mine said, "Look, you're a reasonably bright guy, and you're going to be very sorry if you turn around when you're thirty and you're nothing but a broken-down trombone player." It seemed to me he was right. I couldn't get into Berkeley because I'd flunked Chemistry and Latin in high school and graduated half a year late. But I got into San Jose State on probation. I was twenty-three when I started.

You've written a lot about Los Angeles; is that because it's where you're from or. . . .

Leigh: Well, I've written a lot more than I've published, and you don't know the half of it. L.A. and San Francisco just seem to be the two places where I can comfortably set a book. I haven't really much sense of place, and if I could blame that on being from Southern California I would. It's something extraordinary, L.A. Nobody I know of has ever got a rope round it at all in fiction except for Nathanael West perhaps. I've spent an awful lot of time trying to write a big L.A. novel without succeeding.

Your first book?

Leigh: No, the book I wrote after I published WHAT CAN YOU DO? which I thought of as an extremely modest first novel. I was wildly ambitious. In part of my head I still am. Anyway, the L.A. book took a couple of years' hard work and came out at 691 manuscript pages. With my first book out, I felt I could call myself a writer with less embarrassment, and I got keen on the idea of going down to L.A., isolating myself, really soaking myself in all *that*. So I did, for most of a year, living alone in my friend George Price's mother's cabin in the hills between Malibu and the valley. It got very strange indeed. Christ, if you're living down there with your radio tuned twenty-four hours a day to one of those Top Forty stations, and driving around on those freeways, you get soaked in *something* after awhile. And then that was the year after the first Watts riots, and I was going down to Watts a lot, seeing what I could pick up. On my antennae, I mean.

The book was about a rock station and disc jockeys and exploitation of young talent and young consumers and the, to me, obvious political implications of all this. I knew a little about the business end because I'd worked for a record company and then in a distributor's warehouse. Anyway, the book had seventy characters and half a dozen plots, helicopters wheeling around, and a private army, all tied together by the freeways and God knows what. Nothing, perhaps, or not enough.

It ended in a kind of generalized guerrilla warfare, only in much greater detail than the touch at the end of THE RASMUSSEN DISASTERS. But if you want to write about a civil war situation in the United States, you have to be ready to go all the way with it, and I don't think I know enough. Somebody could write a fine book about it, using the war to expose America's extraordinary virutes and weaknesses under that pressure. Maybe a black writer, but not necessarily. Maybe somebody with Vietnam behind him. But certainly my book got out of hand, and I've never known what to do with it. There were a lot of moments when I was perfectly sure that I could tie *everything* into it and make sense. But for one thing I was writing much too close to the newspapers at the time. I'd always had this feeling that you should be trying to deal with your time, which is *right now*. But unless you're a genius, you run the risk of being dated or simply a bad prophet by the time the book gets in print.

Did THE RASMUSSEN DISASTERS *come out of this book?*

Leigh: Not really.

A portion of it?

Leigh: No, not a word, really. In the big L.A. book I wanted to have *everything*, as I said. RASMUSSEN is much less ambitious. It started out from a scrap of an old short story I never got right— Rasmussen starting his day –plus a good, half-digested idea, which got away from me in the course of the book. But I'm personally fond of it anyway, perhaps because it was such a miserable failure.

My edition of THE RASMUSSEN DISASTERS *was published in England. Was it published in this country?*

Leigh: You'd never know it, babe. Yeah, it was published. I've got a whole box of remaindered U.S. editions downstairs, probably as many as were sold in the City and County of San Francisco. You could say it didn't sell.

Do you worry about sales when you're writing?

Leigh: No, I don't worry about sales when I'm writing. You can feel bad about it, and that's all you *can* do, unless you're an enormously prestigious writer, a big property. I can feel unhappy that RASMUSSEN sold maybe nine hundred and some copies in hardback and there's no paperback, because I think, given my natural bias, that it's a better book than that, better than lots of books that sold far more. To that degree I'm sorry, but so what? As a public fact, it was a bummer. It's out of my hands.

It's not a bummer book.

Leigh: Well, a bummer is a book that bombs. Those are the facts of life. If you can feel good thinking that MOBY DICK sold fewer copies, fine. But you have to believe you're in that class. I have a couple of friends whose novels have sold under a thousand, guys of great dedication and talent who have had that kind of fate. It may cost you money, years of your life, it may cost you God knows what trying to write the best book you know how, and then it gets published, in effect, in Grand Rapids on a rainy midnight, and vanishes without a trace. I was once on a panel discussion at L.A. State, don't ask about what, I think *The Function of the Novel in Modern Life*, that kind of thing, and there was a guy on the panel whose novel had been brought out, by a trade publisher of no particular disrepute, and then had not received one review. Not one. Imagine that. Enough. No more horror stories.

Is it a mark of success when a book comes out in paperback?

Leigh: It's a mark of money, and a chance of being read by a lot more people. If you nourish any hope of making a living at writing, paperbacks seem necessary. There were a few years there when I made a lot of money; no justice in it, of course, or in the pitiful amounts better writers were making those same years. Money is money. You need it to live, and if you can call it success, call it success. I got tired of living on red beans and rice and Grade B Dirties quite a while ago. Those are the cheapest eggs, they probably don't even sell them anymore. I think kids now seem to have a lot more talent for starving, or playing at Holy Poverty. They're a little better organized for it, with this or that sort of communalism. Also they're less troubled by certain guilts. I would never have thought of living communally when I was a kid. I was much too hipped on necessary solitude, poignant isolation, the whole romantic individualistic package. I don't mean to put it down now, either. How did I get to this?

You said RASMUSSEN *started with one idea. What was it?*

Leigh: Simply the brothers, two apparently opposed people, one a hopelessly square suburban husband-and-father, the other an aging beatnik trying to make it as a hippy. I began the book absolutely sure that something made them practically twins, and that that something was important. But I never got a clear conception of it, and I lost my grip and got stuck instead on the idea of the mini-orgy inside the house as an analog to the general situation outside, including the quasi-civil war, an idea which I think I better give up on now.

It sort of struck us both as David's book.

Leigh: Certainly it is, if only in the sense that it's not nearly generous enough to the rest of the family, and the only character for whom any hope is shown is young David. It's from a viewpoint that I make my one feeble stab at recapturing the original idea of the book, but his viewpoint is insufficient to it. I think that instead of finding the necessary sympathy for David's mother and father, what I tried to do, and did reasonably well, was explain how they got the way they are. But that just isn't good enough. I'm still wishing to write about ordinary people, whatever those are, people below the twenty-fifth percentile, any twenty-fifth percentile. People who don't have fantastic love lives. Nelson Algren talks about characters whose lives offer them no alternatives, but I haven't been on the street enough or lived a hard enough life to write with any real authority about characters like that. Still I'm stuck on the idea of writing about characters who, by and large, get discarded as material for fiction. There are just far too many easy ways for self-esteemed "educated" people and "hip" people to look down on maybe sixty percent of the country or more. What they look down on, and lots of novelists and college professors help them, are not those people as they are, but on stupid inaccurate stereotypes. If you want proof of this, read the books of Robert Coles. He didn't make those people up, they're real. It's the ones in our heads, the hard hats, the rednecks, all the baddies, that aren't real. We've been lied to so much by people making money off us that we've taken to lying to ourselves, out of laziness and the desire to feel superior. Quite human. My books have suffered from it, and this whole sermon I just got into is mainly for home consumption.

David Rasmussen is sympathetic, but many of the characters— Rasmussen and Bernie in THE RASMUSSEN DISASTERS, *Phil Fuller in*

WHAT CAN YOU DO?, Mr. Long in DOWNSTAIRS AT RAMSEY'S—*many seem to be either comic or amoral.*

Leigh: Or worse?

Or worse.

Leigh: Christ, there are worse things than comic characters. I better skip the way those adjectives complicate each other for me. An amoral character may be the sign of an uncontrollably moralistic writer, which I may be. Maybe you try to conceal such a thing by trying to be funny. Keeping a tidy head isn't easy. Most of what I've got published I wouldn't care to do any more; that's one reason why it's taking me so long to get another book out. You change, you find fault with what you've done. A lot of the time I'm extremely confused . . .

The tone and humor in RASMUSSEN *were very different from that in* DOWNSTAIRS AT RAMSEY'S—

Leigh: Colder, I'd say.

—But they're both funny books.

Leigh: I'm glad you think so.

Do you think humor is some sort of salvation?

Leigh: Well, sure, I guess so. I'd hate to debate anybody who thought so. But teaching school I try to distinguish between funny language and funny behavior. The kind of humor that arises from the narrator, or the tone, or the clever diction, whatever, saying to the reader, "Look at that silly asshole, isn't he a scream?" is almost always crueller, and, I think, inferior.

I don't mean these cover all bases, or that they aren't often mixed, perhaps marvelously well. Take a really great writer like Faulkner, say. He can get a lot of mileage out of the way his crackerbarrel narrators (Ratliff is a great one) *talk* about other characters. But he also finds and shows you comic behavior, he *sees* what is funny in behavior which someone else, often other characters, miss. Comic diction or comic action. What I'd like to get is people doing things which may strike the reader as funny or humorous without my using a lot of verbal jive gimmicks. Which is another way of saying I want to write better about characters. It's something you have to sort out for yourself, from your own life, from whatever you think your own problems are, from your own affections and rages. It's not easy. I get so God-damned angry with this country, people killing each other all the time. And themselves. There's a few non sequiturs for you.

Let me try to find an example, because I think it's important. A witty book has the potential of being cutting, vicious. I put off reading a book by Randall Jarrell, PICTURES FROM AN INSTITUTION, for years because I'd been told it was a purely bitchy academic novel. Which it is, and so cruel, written like one long 18th-century epigram, or J. V. Cunningham, do you know "Lip"? About a colleague of his, supposedly:

Lip was a man who used his head
He used it when he went to bed
With his friend's wife, or with his friend,
With either sex at either end.

Anyway, the Jarrell book is like that, only two hundred fifty or three hundred pages. That kind of precision. But by God in the end it's a warm, affectionate book. Incredible. You finish and wonder how he did it. That seems to be something to aspire to.

Do you think Evan Connell does that in MRS. BRIDGE?

Leigh: Yeah, in another way he certainly does. That's a book that hits a lot of nerves. It certainly hits mine. But it's written, I'd say, with much more feeling backed up and under control than the Jarrell book. Not more control, mind you. More feeling. MRS. BRIDGE is a real model for that kind of family book. Tremendously dry and restrained. The details do so much. Jesus, you know what must have gone into that book. It must have cost him something, or maybe it freed him, or both. Both or neither. I shouldn't even speculate about it. I don't know the man at all, just met him at a party a couple of months ago, five-second handshake. He seems a very self-sufficient man.

Doesn't the quality you're talking about have a lot to do with avoiding sentimentality?

Leigh: The kind of books we've just been talking about surely do avoid it, but too great a fear of sentimentality produces a tremendous sterility. I think you can't possibly write well if you're too afraid of spilling your guts, of writing what *somebody* might call sentimentality. You've got to be prepared to walk that brink and take your chances on falling over. It's one virtue of techniques. The right one can allow you to find just the right distance for your feelings. But if you're too detached, it becomes too easy, and too attractive, to make fun of people *merely* cruelly. It's a capacity we all have. I know I do. It's a thing you have to keep under control.

Do you prefer to write out of imagination rather than experience?

Leigh: I haven't that much choice. I don't think my own experience is—well, if what you mean is autobiographical writing, I'm not interested. For my taste, there's too much of it. There's a great trend toward the memoir. Okay, *call* it a memoir. I'm not ready to write mine. This may just be taste, or it may be that I simply can't cope with my little bit of experience. Besides, my whole idea of fiction is something else, nothing especially unique about it: you make things up out of what you know, what you see, what you imagine, and it leaves you a certain freedom from history, from what actually happened in time and space. You can make something that never was before.

When you start a book do you start with a character or a situation or an idea, or do you have the end in mind? Where do you begin?

Leigh: Various places. I can run them down for you. The first book, WHAT CAN YOU DO?, was a one-character, first-person book whose voice demanded its point of view. I had the kid talking in my ear, very much like myself, perhaps too much. DOWNSTAIRS AT RAMSEY'S, written bang right after I finished the long L.A. monster, started with a real cliché situation, like *Bachelor Father*, maybe, I've never seen that. Based on a drunken conversation, of which the book contains a perverse version. I couldn't think of how to write it. Then I thought of the old English actor digging it from upstairs. A device, a gimmick, but sent from heaven it felt like. Opened the book right up, and I did the first draft in five weeks. But it began with the situation, and no end in mind. With RASMUSSEN DISASTERS I didn't have the end in mind either. There I wanted to write a book in which I used complete third-person omniscience, going into anybody's head at will and out again. Yeah, you hear a creative-writing teacher sounding off. Anyway, I am very fond of the opening pages of RASMUSSEN because they do just what I wanted them to, go from an astronaut's view of the great globe itself right down to Rasmussen scratching his balls on a Sunday morning. Mind you, I don't think I did so much with the rest of the book, although the entrances and exits are nicely managed. It was a pleasure, and instructive. I loved writing the "all-over-California" passages later on. Something about the voice, and voice is the concept that is really helpful to me, actually to think of the kind of voice or voices. Just like heard human voices. What's the voice going to be like? What's the right voice?

How does the character or the voice develop?

Leigh: I'm not sure my characters do develop the way they are supposed to. Somebody—a friend, I think—told me that my characters were static, but that was okay because I was a comic writer. Mmm. At that point my head shut off the way it used to in late-afternoon seminars at Stanford. Theory . . . oh my . . . But having the end in mind or not is interesting.

I've always been impressed— too impressed, probably—with Faulkner saying that if you do your work right, the characters will stand up and walk, along about page 275, and then all you have to do is take notes on what they do. Now, every year that passes, more of my head says "Bullshit!" It may have worked that way for him, but I've slowly come to terms with the fact that I'm not Faulkner. Oh my, have I!

But I've trusted that saying of his in the past. I liked the openness of working on a book where you only have a general sense of the situation. You go in and work every day and see where it takes you. There's a delicate balance between your control —you're always in charge, but certain imperatives may seem to arise out of the characters even in the most modest books. In RAMSEY's, Hardy Brewster *had* to go to jail, and I fought a pretty good rumble against a couple of editors, one of whom wanted him to marry his teenager in a campy Hollywood wedding chapel. Anyway, that's a particular part of the pleasure of writing novels. I'm a great Raymond Chandler fan, I reread him every couple of years. The first winter I spent in Spain I decided I'd write a Raymond Chandler, and finish it. I mean, I'd started half a dozen when I was a kid. His Bay City is my home town, you know, Santa Monica. So I got the first chapter written, terrific, and a really good situation. Not like Ross Macdonald, who just used Chandler's LADY IN THE LAKE plot over and over and over. Then I realized that to write a Chandler, you've got to begin at the end. Oh definitely. So I laid the whole thing out as well as I could, and got a couple of chapters further and quit out of boredom because I knew exactly where it was going. You have to figure out the properly devious way to get there. Enough false leads, enough shootings and betrayals, all *motivated*, too . . .

Didn't Chandler say, "When you don't know what to do next, have a man come in the door with a gun in his hand"?

Leigh: Yeah. Jesus Christ, you're right! Does that mean that maybe Chandler *didn't* always begin at the end? No, he must have been kidding his own style. But it's a mind-bending possibility. I know *I'd* have to begin at the end. Then when you don't finish you're left with an ending instead of a beginning? I have so many unfinished novels. It comes from loving to begin them too much. I'd love to begin about one a week; that first week is such a joy. If I could sign a contract to provide the first ten pages of a novel, say three times a month for the rest of my life, I'd sign like a shot. But then it would turn into one of those special purgatories, I guess, not to be *allowed* fo finish, a clause in the contract . . .

How do you go about that? Do you set aside a certain time of day, a certain number of hours to write?

Leigh: Yeah, I write every morning. I like to work every day. I feel better, physically, every way. A really compulsive, old-fashioned habit, though I don't see how anybody can write long fiction without such a habit. If I take a day off, it takes an extra day to get back in, so one day is two. And then I like it, I just basically like it. I like the act of getting up in the morning and going in and sitting down at the typewriter.

Has moving around hurt that habit?

Leigh: No, not strictly speaking, I don't think so. Wherever I am, I get up and whack away at the typewriter every day. If I'm not writing anything, my friends get a lot of extra-long letters. I'm fairly numb about where I am. At the same time, I think we stayed in Spain a couple of years too long. Because I couldn't see myself leaving such an apparently perfect set-up. I mean, I had what I'd always wanted, and what most of my contemporaries wanted, and what a few of my students want, perhaps more than a few. A comfortable house, pleasant weather, enough money to live on and unlimited time to write. I wrote all the time practically; I finished three novels and published two of them; I started as many or more other novels and didn't finish them. You know, it was The Writer's Life, a more modest version of Clifford Irving. You say to yourself, "If I can't make it under such ideal conditions, it must be me to blame, and not the place." Might as well leave it at that.

Could you talk a bit about the problems a writer has once he's published?

Leigh: Yeah, they're nowhere near as bad as the problems a writer has before he's published. Ask me another one like that.

I was thinking about problems with editors and publishers.

Leigh: Well, writers can sit around telling horror stories about editors and publishers all night long, and I have my share; but a lot of them are about other writers because on the whole, I've been very well treated. I've had fantastic luck; that seems an objective fact. I'm no kind of important writer; I haven't published a really impressive book; but I've made a lot of money, mainly by having a great agent: two, in fact, one in New York and one in London.

Most of the money came from movie rights, didn't it?

Leigh: From movie rights and from paperbacks, yeah. For that, somebody has to think you're commercial. I'm afraid I may have disappointed a few folks along those lines. I haven't asked.

Which books sold to the movies?

Leigh: The first two. But RAMSEY'S was scrapped for a tax credit when some conglomerate bought Warner Brothers, it's one of the little favors we do for corporations in this country, like oil depletion. And the movie they made from WHAT CAN YOU DO? found its way onto several Worst Ten lists last year. Came out under the title MAKING IT. Wishful thinking. THE NEW YORKER had a great one-liner: "This film was made from a novel called WHAT CAN YOU DO? What you can do is not go."

But you went?

Leigh: Had to. I caught it at the Times, Stockton and Broadway, you know? Ninety-nine cents, and I was robbed. But I didn't offer the studio the money back. As it turned out they didn't need it. The producer just went ahead and made "The Godfather."

Did you mean a little while ago that you've had no troubles with editors and publishers? What about a writer's relationship with his editors? You mentioned that you had to argue over the end of RAMSEY'S.

Leigh: Let me try and sort that out. Publishers are corporations run for profit. They're companies that employ editors. A writer, unless he's a pure hack, a money machine—and there aren't nearly as many of those as you might think—a writer is bound to have certain built-in, head-on conflicts of interest with publishers if not editors necessarily. Each regards the other as a means to an end, like one of those love affairs you read about where two people agree more or less amicably to use each other, "without getting involved," right? Each one hopes to get what he wants and escape intact. But it's not surprising that a little love and a lot of hate arise in the process: love when the other party serves you well, hate when he doesn't, etc.

I've only had one American publisher, and the same is almost true in England, where the lady who edited my first book at one publisher went on to publish my second and third herself with her own company. So, you see where I'm headed in such a round-about way. If you ask someone who is happily married how much he and his wife fight, you mustn't expect too much scandal. The difference of opinion I mentioned over RAMSEY's—well, look, in that case either I had my way or I'd have taken the book elsewhere. I got my way, and that was that. But I've also had the experience of absolutely first-rate editing, from a great lady named Elizabeth Lawrence, now retired at Harper & Row after many years there. Once you've had that, you are in no position to be pigheaded about editors in general. They are people who may help you or they may not. If you seem stuck with one you feel strongly doesn't dig what you're up to, you or your agent can try to switch you to another one. Or to another publisher. I hate to generalize from my own experience. As somebody who takes money for teaching writing courses, I know how many different ways different people's egos get caught in the blades. I know I wouldn't care to be an editor, constantly walking that wire between his sense of what is of literary value and his awareness of the cost accountants. Many don't walk that wire, of course, but I know a few that do.

Do editors read all the manuscripts they get?

Leigh: I'm in no position to say for sure. What I suspect is that unless you have a very good entree, or an agent, or both, that is if you just wrap up a manuscript and mail it to a publisher cold, it's very likely going to be read by a young lady from Sweetbriar or Smith or Vassar who maybe has a little money of her own and is working as an editorial assistant for coolie wages so she can get into publishing. And she may have taste, and she may not, but she packs no weight. Only if she likes it, she'll recommend it to a senior editor, and if *he* likes it, something might happen. In some houses a strong editor can accept a book on his own and see it through. In a good many—more all the time, I'd guess—it takes some sort of committee approval, with cost accountants on the committee.

My first book was apparently accepted by a publisher that used a committee system. There were five fiction editors, and they voted unanimously to publish it. I was in Mexico at the time. An airmail letter came from the woman who was boss fiction editor, and we got right into the tequila, ignoring the last sentence, something like "Of course Mr. M. will have to okay it when he gets back from vacation, but we don't expect that to be a problem." Mr. M. is the president of the company. He comes back, reads a couple of pages and says he'd resign before he'd publish such garbage. I got a sad letter from the five editors saying they'd been outvoted. But that book was turned down at eleven places before it was accepted.

WHAT CAN YOU DO?

Leigh: Yes.

You had an agent at the time?

Leigh: Yes, Anne Curtis-Brown. Very sweet woman. She had more faith in the book than I did. She died seven years ago.

When one book is accepted, do you get committed for another?

Leigh: In the standard contract what they actually buy is an option to look at your next book first. First refusal rights, I think they call it. You aren't normally committed to write another book nor are they to publish it, but if you do write it, they get the first look. Publishers will sometimes publish a book of which they don't think at all highly to keep an option on what the writer might do next, if they think he is promising. At least they used to. Before I got my first contract from Harper, Elizabeth Lawrence was in San Francisco, and she took me to lunch, to decide, she told me later, whether I was a one-book writer or not. WHAT CAN YOU DO? could easily have been a one-shot book. I saw that.

Are you really interested in diversity? Your three published books are so different.

Leigh: I'm glad you think so. I get more ideas for books than I've ever been able to carry out, by a ratio of eight or ten to one, at least. I'm not what I think of as really accomplished, technically, but I like to try different things. I've heard Wright Morris say that when he's three-quarters of the way through one book, he sees the next one winking at him over his shoulder. *Her* shoulder, I think he said. Maybe the Bitch Mailer is always talking about, I wouldn't know. But I usually do finish a book with some idea of the next one, and the next one is always different. I just haven't been finishing enough books the last few years before starting on the next one. What do you figure it is? Early middle-aged restlessness? Gemini flightiness?

Are you into astrology?

Leigh: No, man, I went to college in the Fifties! I've been working on a book with an astrological grandma in it, for which I read Linda Goodman and Sydney Omarr, that's all. Ah, well, what the hell, I'm an agnostic not an atheist. And three separate times in my life ladies who couldn't *possibly* have known, no way in the world, three times I've been pegged as a Gemini first crack. That's eleven-to-one odds parlayed three times. I have a good friend who says astrology is "one more grid," and I guess I go along with that.

This book with the grandma in it, is it a novel?

Leigh: For want of a better name, a short novel. I've had hints I should try a non-fiction book, but I was an indifferent journalist and a half-hearted scholar, so I think I'll stick to novels, even though the demand for them may fall off a bit.

None of your three published novels were especially long, and you're working on a short novel now, but earlier, talking about the big L.A. novel, you said you wanted to write a book that had everything in it. Do you still want to write big novels?

Leigh: I've written two long novels, if we mean big that way. Both unpublished, in fact both unsubmitted. What is it about Americans that they want to write big books? Even if you know better, you may still want to write a big book. The Great American Novel—you know that old gag?—would just have to be seven to eight hundred pages long at least, wouldn't it? I even think that what most people mean, particularly non-writers, if they mean anything by the Great American Novel, has already been written. U.S.A. It's got everything in it, how many decades of history and eight thousand characters, the "newsreel" business, and those marvelous short biographies. Sartre says somewhere that it's the greatest novel of the twentieth century, and practically nobody reads it any more. The one time I tried to teach it, my students fell asleep, though Dos Passos shouldn't take that rap.

Do you prefer a small perfect work?

Leigh: No, I prefer a big perfect work. I even prefer a big imperfect work. It's a bit stupid to compare THE POSSESSED with, say, GATSBY or MADAME BOVARY, but there's an important sense in which I like THE POSSESSED more. Say more rather than better. This is an emotional preference, at the very least a very special respect for the writer who takes a big cut. Look, if you spend your life writing, you've got that much time to cut back and pare down your ambitions to match what you achieve. Failure makes people timid. The clichés grow particularly thick around here: better to have loved and lost, etc. A distinct sort of boldness is required. I know a man who is one of those hard-luck writers. He's written at least eight novels that I know of, possibly a dozen by now. Of those he published two, and nothing happened with either of them. As a result of what has now been close to twenty-five years of much more rejection and disregard than acceptance, and no appreciation at all, his ambitions have shrunk. Understandably, you might say. And one of the things he has always had is a really extraordinary mind—no one like him in the world—and an extraordinary ability to conceive big worthwhile projects. Plus a tireless devotion to the necessary discipline of writing long fiction. The details of his particular bad luck, with agents and editors and publishers, Christ, they would make a fifty-page horror story. He never quite fit any of the going molds; his uniqueness was never seen and it cost him. Having had to literally watch someone you know shrinking in the dimension where he was strongest, well, it's had the effect on me of making me see the steady waste of his ambition as the loss of something precious. The ambition itself is precious, intrinsically. Americans have thought so. It's not entirely a bad thing in the nation's character, a constant awareness of how far you fall short. Not that all Americans possess it.

That strikes a chord in me, the idea that the conception itself, even if followed by failure, is worth something—

Leigh: I simply believe it. Lots of people believe it. Without the conception, technique is helpless, and so on. On that level it's un arguable. It's an idea you could probably trace out historically— it's a version of "Think Big!" "Go West, Young Man!" and so forth. You could say that the idea of doing things on a big scale leads to disasters like Vietnam. But we're talking about writing books. Being a teacher of writing, and knowing something about the editing process, I've come to feel that most of it can't help being reductive. I mean, for every time a teacher really feels comfortable encouraging a student to expand something, there must be fifty times when one feels required, not out of cowardice or meanness but just the necessity of trying to be constructive—ha! one feels required to suggest that the student cut something out. That can't help but militate in the direction of smaller conceptions. Unless maybe it makes the student explode and write a three thousand-page novel called OF LIFE AND DEATH.

Is the combination of teaching writing and writing yourself a problem for you?

Leigh: Sure. Too often, and I doubt that I'm unique this way, they seem to tap the same pool of energy. But I have a lot of compromise in my nature, like it or not, and I've worked at enough other jobs to realize that writing would combine worse with anything else I might be doing. And then I need to be busy. I'm not talented at leisure. And on top of that, I like teaching. My father was an actor; I used to be a musician: there may be that bit of performing in the family genes.

What kind of work is coming out of the best students you have?

Leigh: The best I've ever seen. As a whole, I mean, because I've had a few fantastically good students in the past, too. What there doesn't seem to be much of anymore is a middle. Students seem to be either rather mature and responsible people—I often wonder what I can teach them—or hopeless and misguided and illiterate, sometimes charming, but not often. Not much of a middle—students you might hope to be slow developers but hopeful. I see a certain amount of what I suppose is meant to be experimental stuff, rigidly intense, maybe incoherent. Some science-y fiction, some Tolkien-y fantasy. Giant mushrooms and God having conversations and nothing is supposed to mean much, or *anything* can mean *everything*—I've said too much already.

But it's shifted a lot?

Leigh: In six years? Well, yeah, and doubtless I've shifted some, too. I'd say it seems to have become a little more traditional or conservative, but they're such horrible words locally. Say that quite a few students seem to be more aware of more possibilities—what fiction *has* done and thus *can* do. And then, the guys that have been in Vietnam are an extraordinary new presence out there. I'm not trying to send up a balloon or anything, only to note that in 1966 the year I left, there were not that many veterans in evidence, and now—well, they are in evidence, they're really something else. I'm talking about three, four, maybe five guys. I know there are more. They're literate or well on their way to being so; obviously they have read a lot for pleasure. They've kissed off so many things. Nobody is too likely to tell them that dropping a pill is going to make them geniuses. They've seen the war. They tend to be fairly considerate of younger, less experienced students, very focussed on what they are doing, not at all patient with bullshit. And there must be a few more coming . . .

What about your students' taste in fiction?

Leigh: It divides. Some students, particularly graduates—and they come from all over the country, you know—some of them have picked up, or given themselves, pretty flossy educations, they've read very widely, in literature and elsewhere. Others, well, Christ, they are depressingly predictable. Vonnegut and Herman Hesse, Richard Brautigan. Maybe the I CHING or the latest single-volume total instant cosmic education. Whatever there are ten stacks of at City Lights or the Tides. The ones who have read almost invariably write better than those who haven't. Well, of course. In a language like English, if you haven't read, maybe literally can't read because your mind is so messed up, how can you write? You've got no idea what the language can do. You haven't a clue about what a good novel or story or poem is. I've been hearing about the "natural" all my life and have never met him. When I was a whole lot younger, I was told once or twice that I was he, and of course it was a lie.

How do your best students feel about the possibility of becoming teacher-writers? When I was going through the B.A. out there, it seemed like a logical progression: the B.A., the M.A., the teaching job, and writing. But now that seems almost impossible.

Leigh: I gather that my best students feel various ways, though quite strongly. I know one who could have breezed through grad. school who could just barely stand to finish this year and get his B.A. before splitting. Others have been out there, maybe have families, and see the combination as the best game in town, despite its drawbacks. As a group I guess you could say they feel resigned, bitter perhaps, but not suicidal. Not too bad a way to feel in 1972, I'd say. Jesus, look at me: when I was an undergraduate I said, "I'll never go to grad school." I got a scholarship and went to grad school, where I said, "I'll never teach." Then I got offered a job, and I said, "Well, I'll never teach writing." How can you trust a guy like that?

Do you think a lot of your students will continue with their writing?

Leigh: No. I think you really need a lifetime virus infection, the odds are so horrible. And the drop-out rate has always been high. I know that six to eight years ago I used to think that some of the best student writers gave up because they were such nice people. Their girls got pregnant or their parents got sick. Somebody had to be taken care of, and they'd quit to take a job that you knew would never let them write. Girls and women may have intense bursts of doing fine work and then quit forever, typically to get married or have kids, though this may sound sexist. And then some of them got into dope and couldn't handle it. Only a relatively small number of people actually ever got anything published. I really believe in "mute inglorious Miltons." I have no choice but to. But people know all this, or they find it out, and they go ahead, some of them. I have to believe that you can't easily kill off a good writer who has to write. For myself I've come to believe in the compulsion to write as a necessity, because what else is going to keep you going when there are so many alternatives? It's extremely hard to make a living and to write on the side. There's so much you have to give up, and why should you? Even so, we produce books like popcorn, and most of them a lot less filling. Even in the Book of ECCLESIASTES, what does it say? How many centuries before Gutenburg? It says, "Of the making of books there is no end, and much study is a weariness of the flesh."

Since our interview the Leighs returned to Europe for a year and then came back to San Francisco where Jim teaches creative writing classes full-time at San Francisco State University. They have bought a house on Noe Street in San Francisco and have a second child, Alyssia Zdena. Jim's fourth novel, NO MAN'S LAND, was published in the Summer of 1975 by The Alison Press/Secker and Warburg in London, and he has completed a final retyping job on a long novel he completed in 1973 which soon will be sent to New York. He is currently at work on a sixth novel.

DT

NOVELS

What Can You Do? New York: Harper & Row, 1965. (Dell, 1966.)

Downstairs at Ramsey's. New York: Harper & Row, 1968. (Bantam Books, 1969.)

The Rasmussen Disasters. New York: Harper & Row, 1969.

No Man's Land. London: The Alison Press/Secker and Warburg, 1975.

Janet Lewis

Janet Lewis is a living example of
the idea that the very best writers are often those who, at first, are
most ignored by the general public. A widow, she lives with a
ferocious looking, but very friendly English bulldog. Her house is
white stucco, a small house in a modest Los Altos neighborhood.
Inside, everything is in shadow. The trees and the bushes outside in
the overgrown garden and the heavy curtains transform daylight
into twilight. There is the smell of fine, old furniture and the
outline of many books in their cases along the walls.

Miss Lewis is a lean, strong-featured woman dressed in pants,
white blouse, and wool cardigan. She sits in the living room and
discusses her work in a precise, resonant voice. Her sentences flow
out polished and whole, without apparent effort, as if everything

were obvious. This may be true, but is nevertheless deceptive. Her best books can be read, and enjoyed, on many different levels: as exciting mysteries, colorful historical romances, penetrating psychological studies, and ultimately, as explorations of man's moral position in the universe and the tenacious dignity of the human spirit. While novels by richer and more famous writers are forgotten, hers radiate, long after they are put down, a quiet, powerful, almost ascetic, beauty.

RH

When did you first start writing?

Lewis: I started writing when I was in high school. My first published poems were in POETRY in June, 1920. My first story, which was written in 1922, came out quite some years later in THE BOOKMAN.

Why did you want to be a writer?

Lewis: It seemed to be the only thing I could do better than other things. My father was an English teacher, and he was also a novelist. He wrote very good poetry too. I grew up thinking that writing was a great thing, naturally.

Did you want to be a poet first?

Lewis: Yes, but you can't sell poetry much, and I discovered I could occasionally sell a story.

Is poetry more difficult to write?

Lewis: Yes.

Why?

Lewis: One writes less good poetry in a lifetime than one writes fiction. It is more concentrated; it has to be better.

How did you become interested in writing historical novels?

Lewis: Well, the first historical novel, THE INVASION, I was interested in because I knew the people. Miss Molly Johnson and Howard Johnson, who were characters that appear toward the end of the book, I knew when I was a little girl. During summer vacations, I grew up hearing them tell stories around campfires about their grandmother, Neengay, who was the Indian woman in the story, and their grandfather, John Johnson. When I began doing short stories, I thought, "I'll do a sketch of Miss Molly." I found out pretty soon that I had to do not only Miss Molly, but her ancestors. After that, I was up to my neck.

In THE INVASION you include actual letters written by the historical characters. The book is half-documentary, half-fiction. What made you choose this form?

Lewis: I started to tell the truth, and I wanted to make it as complete as possible, so I treated it as if it were a story. There's nothing in THE INVASION that isn't true as far as I could verify it. I found out later that there were some mistakes.

How did you do the research for that book?

Lewis: Miss Molly's brothers, Howard Lewis Johnson and William Johnson, sent me things. My father was still living in Michigan in the summers and did a great many things for me. Governor Chase Osborne lent me books. Oh, I had splendid help long distance.

What are the advantages in writing historical novels?

Lewis: You know the end. Also, it has a shape.

How much of that shape is fact, and how much is fiction?

Lewis: The essential shape is fact. You know what happens and to whom it happens. But why it happens, you don't know until you can imagine inside these people, and then you have your characters and your plot. It's very hard writing about contemporary things: there's so much. It's very hard to get the outline and disregard the unnecessary stuff. That's why I had so much trouble with my non-historical novel, AGAINST A DARKENING SKY, I'm sure. The plot of the novel is very, very slight, really; and my interest was in the people and in the scene, but I had to hang it on some line of action.

Are there any disadvantages in writing historical novels?

Lewis: Yes. You're not there, you weren't there. You have to make it up, and sometimes this is difficult.

How do you go about it?

Lewis: You never can be sure that you're really getting the feeling of it. But if you read the contemporary things, like the memoirs of the Duc de St. Simon, you get the immediate description of seventeenth century Frenchmen. As somebody working at a distance, you have to fill in sometimes.

Do you do a lot of research?

Lewis: I did a lot of research for THE GHOST OF MONSIEUR SCARRON. I had maps of Paris for the period I was working on that were bigger than that rug. The Louvre prints fresh ones from the originals, and a friend of mine sent me some. When I got to Paris, I knew the Paris of 1690 better than the Paris of 1951. I'd go down a street and find that something had changed.

Where do you begin your research?

Lewis: Where do I begin? For THE WIFE OF MARTIN GUERRE, I began by reading a book on the Ancien Régime by Frantz Funck-Brentano that had a lot of stories in it and lots of quotes from contemporary writers that gave a feeling of life then. I read guide books. I talked to a skier from Luchon to find out how the snow was in the Pyrenees. And I had an old French woman as a neighbor here with whom I used to visit. She gave me the whole episode of the housekeeper's killing of the doves. Do you remember that?

Yes. Where Bertrande feels her strength is ebbing away as she sees the dove's blood dripping into the pan.

Lewis: It happened almost exactly that way. When I was writing the novel, I remembered my neighbor—if you want to call that research—but this is where the material came from: as much from things that happened or from people I knew or from my having been to France once, as from books, and I think this is what brings it to life.

With these things that provide atmosphere and a sense of realism, is the problem to decide what to leave out, or what to include?

Lewis: Both: if you get too much, then you have to decide what to leave out. Sometimes you have to build up. You hunt around for material to reinforce what you want.

You found the plots for THE WIFE OF MARTIN GUERRE, THE TRIAL OF SOREN QVIST, and THE GHOST OF MONSIEUR SCARRON in a book called FAMOUS CASES OF CIRCUMSTANTIAL EVIDENCE. Was this a matter of convenience, or were there other reasons?

Lewis: I had the book. I went through and found THE WIFE OF MARTIN GUERRE, which I thought was particularly interesting. I took notes on the two others, just on the chance that I might want to use them some day, but it was a long time before I went back to them.

What interested you the most about the case of Martin Guerre? Was it the strange circumstances which allowed an imposter to be accepted as Martin by Martin's whole family, including his wife, Bertrande? Or was it Bertrande's reasons for changing her mind and accusing a man she loved of being an imposter?

Lewis: The question of when she changed her mind, and why she changed her mind. There wasn't a great deal given in Phillips. I say "Phillips" because the name of the book is FAMOUS CASES OF CIRCUMSTANTIAL EVIDENCE with an essay by Phillips on evidence. I have to go back to the beginning.

Please do.

Lewis: The original story was told by Jean de Coras. He was one of the judges at the trial and wrote it down when it was still fresh in his mind. Then it went into a number of editions and was translated into Dutch, and I don't know what else. Then, of course, it went out of print. Before that, somebody read it and made a résumé in something called CAUSES CÉLÈBRES. It's rather a brief summary of the case. The CAUSES CÉLÈBRES I found over at Stanford years after I finished the book. From the CAUSES CÉLÈBRES somebody had got hold of it and translated it into English. This went into the collection of FAMOUS CASES with a couple of mistakes in translation which changed the implications of the story a little, as I found out afterwards. So, by the time I got it, it was pretty much second hand, decidedly second hand. I had to fill in things. It wasn't until a few years ago that I saw a Xerox of the original story and found out where I'd guessed wrong—many years too late to change it.

Would you have changed it if you could have?

Lewis: If I were doing it now, it would be a different story, yes. Although it's still possible that I was right in the main.

What would you change?

Lewis: I would change Uncle Pierre, who was a great help in the story, and who was obviously a villain in the real thing.

Whereas, in your version, he helps Bertrande, not because it is a way of legally controlling Martin's property if the man were proved to be an imposter, but because he honestly believes his niece?

Lewis: Yes.

And that's what you would change?

Lewis: I'm afraid I would have to because that's the one thing that's obviously wrong. In the version I had, it mentioned the death of the father. It did not explain that Pierre then married Bertrande's mother and controlled the farm that way. There's an incident in which Pierre accused Martin of something, I've forgotten just what, and had him arrested before there was any question of Martin's being an imposter. The case came up before the judges, and they said that there's nothing to this and turned him loose again. Now that I know a little more, I can see that Bertrande was forced by Pierre to accuse the imposter. There's also evidence in the story by Jean de Coras that she was quite devoted to young Martin before he went away.

Do you believe the historical novelist should stay as close to history as possible?

Lewis: I feel that I would want to stay as close as possible. This would be my interest in it. There are lots of historical novels which are very good and roam very far from the facts, I'm sure. Had I known Pierre was a villain, I would have had a much more complicated story on my hands, and it might not have worked so well. I think, perhaps, I was lucky I didn't know too much.

You would have felt compelled to tell the truth, even though it might have destroyed the story?

Lewis: I'm afraid I would . . .

Earlier, you said that you know what happens and to whom it happens, but not why it happens. In THE WIFE OF MARTIN GUERRE *how did you go about creating Bertrande's emotions and motivations?*

Lewis: Well, you take what facts there are and try to imagine what you would have done in the same circumstances, no?

Would you have accused a man who loved you, and whom you loved, because he was posing as your husband?

Lewis: I couldn't figure her doing anything other than what she did in my story. In FAMOUS CASES the last two speeches in the trial are quoted and not changed from the original French. It is from those two speeches—the one that the real Martin Guerre makes when he comes home and refuses her and the speech Bertrande makes to him justifying herself, explaining herself—those were the two speeches from which I had to build up the characters. Those are the facts. So, I took Bertrande's speech to the judges, which was the way she wanted to be considered, and from that created a Bertrande who was the woman she wanted to be. I didn't realize until many years later that, perhaps, she wasn't that woman. But nobody can tell who she was, really.

A female friend of mine, commenting on Bertrande, said she was a fool. . . .

Lewis: The contemporary reactions are very amusing. Most of them are impatient with her. They say, "Why didn't she take what she had?" and so forth. Most Catholic readers agree that this was the way she should have acted. They understand that. Although, in the beginning, she was overwhelmed and very happy, just the way I did it in the book, as soon as suspicion comes in the thing is poisoned, and she would want to get out of it.

When you go about creating your characters, do they ever run away with you, even though you have the end in mind?

Lewis: Your characters can't run away with you when you know what they are going to do. I mean, they are fated to do, you see, what they have done. They have to move toward their own destiny.

THE WIFE OF MARTIN GUERRE *seems such a perfect book; did you have it very carefully blocked out before writing it?*

Lewis: I wrote it as a long short story. It was a pretty incredible story, and nobody wanted it. My husband said, "It's worth working on. Why don't you fill it in and make it longer." So, that's what I did. I already had an outline to work from.

Do you usually work from an outline?

Lewis: I make an outline in my head.

How long does writing a book take after you have the outline in mind?

Lewis: That's impossible to answer. Different stories take different lengths of time.

How long did THE WIFE OF MARTIN GUERRE *take?*

Lewis: Not very long. I wrote it twice, and a half year elapsed between the first and second versions.

Did you work every day?

Lewis: Every school day, after the family was out of the house.

How long could you spend writing?

Lewis: About two or three hours in the morning. You get the family off to school, and then you have a few hours before it's time to get lunch or do something else. In the afternoons I never could do anything.

In THE WIFE OF MARTIN GUERRE, THE TRIAL OF SOREN QVIST, *and* THE GHOST OF MONSIEUR SCARRON *the basically good characters suffer. Why?*

Lewis: This is natural because theirs were cases of circumstantial evidence, and the characters that are recorded in that book are almost always victims.

Is this a philosophical center of your work?

Lewis: I don't work like that. I don't say, "I will now write a theme of innocence and suffering." I start with a person and then work out the implications. I'm concerned with seeing why a person acts in certain ways. If you've got a sufficiently complicated character, you can get involved with philosophies, of course.

You mentioned that Catholic readers understood Bertrande's actions, but that many modern readers don't. What do you think is the reason for this?

Lewis: Well, you see, France at that time was Catholic. Bertrande lived in a world where there were moral standards. Her way was marked out for her; it was pretty clear. Now the kids have entirely different notions. Infidelity means nothing any more. And there's been Pirandello and all the implications from that state of mind.

Lewis: I think my favorite is THE INVASION. I think SOREN QVIST is a better book than THE WIFE OF MARTINE GUERRE, and I hope THE GHOST OF MONSIEUR SCARRON is a better book than SOREN QVIST, but I can't tell.

Why do you think SOREN QVIST *is better than* THE WIFE?

Lewis: It's more complicated. It has a more complicated character and involves more lines of thought. Soren Qvist is essentially trying to save God, so he's part of a permanent tradition.

So, he refuses to escape from jail even though he has the opportunity and hangs for a crime he didn't commit. Is the idea that he does this in order to save his faith implied in FAMOUS CASES OF CIRCUMSTANTIAL EVIDENCE, *or was it your own creation?*

Lewis: Mine. I'm sure it wasn't implied. As I worked on it, it seemed to me this is what he is doing. The first part ends with: "Why did he do it?" "Why did he let them kill him?" As I thought it over, I saw that he was saving his faith in God.

Have you been influenced by other writers who have written historical novels?

Lewis: I've been influenced by all kinds of writers. As to especially historical novelists, I don't know. I remember trying to read Dumas when I was working on these books, and I found it impossible. I couldn't read Scott either. They used a different approach, so they didn't help. But all good writers influence one. I'm very fond of Colette and Isak Dinesen. I enjoy Mary Renault very much, and lots of American writers: Katherine Anne Porter and Caroline Gordon.

How do you go about revising?

Lewis: Just go. If you can figure what's wrong, you work on it.

Do you do a lot of rewriting?

Lewis: Yes, I do an awful lot of rewriting. I'm likely to rewrite the whole thing, though not sentence by sentence.

Do you finish the whole completely once, and then rewrite the whole thing again?

Lewis: That's what I have done, yes.

Rather than rewrite a chapter as you go along?

Lewis: No, that doesn't work so well, and if you try rewriting bits of sentences or bits of paragraphs, you break the rhythm of the whole thing.

Does the rewrite usually take longer than the original for you?

Lewis: I don't know. Perhaps the same length of time. It depends on how much rewriting there is to do. I don't remember rewriting THE WIFE OF MARTIN GUERRE more than one time. SOREN QVIST I wrote as another long, short story and sent it off somewhere and got it back right away. "This is impossible," they said. Then, one day I just decided to learn something about Jutland and try to do it properly. I did that mostly in one draft and just a little going over afterwards.

How much are you aware of style and technical considerations when you're writing, the structure and flow of individual sentences, and this larger rhythm you spoke of earlier?

Lewis: The rhythm of the action, that's just your feeling for the story.

You agree with Aristotle that plot is the soul of tragedy?

Lewis: It's the essential; something has to happen. One of the editors of THE SATURDAY EVENING POST, Ernie Brandt, I guess, said once, "In a story, something happens." Of course, some events are more important than others.

Your style certainly isn't elaborate. . . .

Lewis: No, it's supposed to be transparent. That was the hope: that you would see what was being told and not get hung up on the way it was being told.

Does this come from the discipline of writing poetry?

Lewis: I'm sure it does. My father was very severe. He was a great stylist. Maybe his novels are not very good as novels, but his style is wonderful. And then, of course, I worked with my husband. He was also strict. I think I did learn my prose style from writing poetry.

Have you ever had the temptation to use some device like interior monologue?

Lewis: Not much. It's very wasteful; I mean it takes a lot of space. If you want to be direct and get on with your story, I think you do better without interior monologue.

What about using the first person?

Lewis: I did do one historical thing in the first person about the American explorers after THE INVASION. I threw it away. It wasn't very successful. I imitated the eighteenth-century manner, the way an eighteenth-century woman would have talked. If you stay outside your character, you can be much freer. You can comment on her, you can move around, you can talk about other people. I don't know. This is one of the great debatable questions.

Would you talk a bit about your teaching at Stanford? Do you think writing can be taught?

Lewis: The writer can be helped. The writer needs people to talk to and bounce his ideas off of. He needs a reaction. There is a great deal that can be taught.

For example?

Lewis: For example, the language. Lots of young writers don't have as large a language as they think they have. The trouble with them now is that they're anti-intellectual. They don't want to have a proper English. They want to use their own manufactured language or the vernacular. This made it hard to teach sometimes. And, if you're going to write poetry, you should know English at least and maybe another language, too. My husband had a nice example. He said, "Joe Louis was a great boxer, but he had a technique, and he trained. He was disciplined. And this, added to his natural gift made him great. Even if you're gifted, it's just as well to have the skills to go with your gift."

How do you go about teaching those skills?

Lewis. I began teaching late after I had been a writer and not a teacher. The thing to do is to get the students to write, and then you have something specific to talk about. Then you see what it is they were trying to do and what they're capable of that they hadn't suspected, things of that sort, finding out what their blocks were and what their gifts were.

Did you give your students writing assignments?

Lewis: Oh, rather. I made them work every day.

Specific assignments?

Lewis: Well, in Narration Five, which was the first course after Freshman English, I gave them specific assignments for short themes and turned them loose with two long papers, or stories. I specified that one of these should be factual, something that actually happened to them, and the other could be anything they wanted to do. Invariably, the factual one was more interesting than the invented one.

Why? Do you believe facts are more interesting than fiction?

Lewis: Not necessarily. God knows I've done enough inventing on my own, but the young writer observing his own life will come up with something more interesting, fresher, than if he sits down and invents something. His invention is not as good as the universe before him.

Then the ability to create comes or increases with age and experience?

Lewis: I think what you do if you're a writer is to observe and gradually merge your observations into something new. If you stick too closely to the observed, of course, you're likely to remain a reporter, or historian, or—what do you call it?—a memorialist. But if you want to create character, you take qualities and put them together in a new person. Then you have new events which are created by new characters. But if you don't start with something real, then your final subject doesn't have any reality.

Do you think reading fiction or non-fiction is a better jumping-off point for the novelist? Which have you read more of?

Lewis: A writer has to read fiction, but if he reads nothing but fiction, I don't think it helps. You have to read some non-fiction to get your material and to know the world you live in. I heard Jessamyn West talking at Stanford once. She said that writers would rather read than anything, but if they're going to write, they can't read all the time. So actually, my reading has been very limited. I haven't read the great long novels. If you're writing historical novels and reading the letters of Mme. de Sevigny or the Memoirs of the Duc de St. Simon, that's necessary and gives you what you need.

In your books you seem to have great compassion for your characters. Do you think this is important in writing?

Lewis: I would find it very difficult to write a book about people for whom I had no concern, no feeling.

Do you think this may be a weakness in much contemporary fiction, especially fiction in the Sixties?

Lewis: I think it might well be. Maybe it's just not contemporary. There are books which seem more witty than concerned with human life.

Considering your feeling about your characters, I was wondering what you thought of the works of Nabokov or Celine, for example?

Lewis: Celine, I've not read, and I haven't read Genêt. Nabokov is immensely gifted, enormously gifted. The book of his I like best is THE REAL LIFE OF SEBASTIAN KNIGHT. LOLITA is a great spoof and take-off in which he lets himself be revenged on all sorts of annoyances in this country. It's a tremendous tour-de-force, but it's not my favorite book. I haven't read the others, PALE FIRE, and so on.

Do you like Sartre?

Lewis: I don't like Sartre.

Literarily or philosophically?

Lewis: Philosophically or temperamentally or something. He's very clever; he's very skillful. He writes good dramas, but I don't like his fundamental point of view. I like Camus.

Would it be possible to write a contemporary WIFE OF MARTIN GUERRE or SOREN QVIST? Do people like that still exist?

Lewis: Yes, I'm sure they still exist.

In a preface to THE TRIAL OF SOREN QVIST you said, "He is one of a great company of men and women who have preferred to lose their lives rather than accept a universe without plan or without meaning." Do you still believe this?

Lewis: I think that's true. All the great religionists feel that it's more important to have a universe that makes sense than to continue to exist in a chaotic world. Wouldn't you agree?

Even if, in fact, the universe doesn't make sense?

Lewis: They would rather be burned at the stake.

Are you writing now?

Lewis: A little.

Are you planning another book?

Lewis: No, a novel takes too much energy and concentration.

Many writers and critics—Evan Connell and Donald Davie, to name a couple—admire your work greatly. Yet, you are not widely known. What is your reaction to this?

Lewis: I think I've had as much recognition as I need and probably as much as I deserve.

NOVELS

The Invasion. New York: Harcourt, Brace & Company, 1932. Published both in hardback and paperback by Alan Swallow, 1964.

The Wife of Martin Guerre. San Francisco: The Colt Press, 1941. (Alan Swallow, 1947. Appeared in ANCHOR IN THE SEA.) Published both in hardback and paperback by Alan Swallow, 1959.

Against a Darkening Sky. New York: Doubleday & Company, 1943.

The Trial of Soren Qvist. New York: Doubleday & Company, 1947. (Alan Swallow, 1959.)

The Ghost of Monsieur Scarron. New York: Doubleday & Company, 1959. (Alan Swallow, 1965.)

SHORT STORIES

Goodbye Son, and Other Stories. New York: Doubleday & Company, 1946.

POETRY AND VERSE

The Indians in the Woods. Bonn: Monroe Wheeler, 1922.

The Wheel in Mid-Summer. Lynn, Mass: Lone Gull Press, 1927.

The Earthbound. Aurora, New York: Wells College, Press, 1946.

Poems 1934–1944. Denver: Alan Swallow, 1950. (Alan Swallow, 1950.)

CHILDREN'S BOOKS

The Adventures of Ollie Ostrich. New York: Doubleday & Company, 1923. [With illustrations by Fay Turpin.]

Keiko's Bubble. New York: Doubleday & Company, 1961. [Illustrated by Kazue Mizumura.]

OTHER

The Wife of Martin Guerre [Libretto]. Denver: Alan Swallow, 1958.

Wallace Stegner

Wallace Stegner has published twenty books, including fiction and nonfiction. In 1972 he won the Pulitzer Prize for his novel, ANGLE OF REPOSE. In addition, he was the head of Stanford University's creative writing program for over twenty years. Now retired from full-time teaching, he continues to write at his home in Los Altos Hills. It is a contemporary home with a sweeping view of the Coast Range.

Dressed casually in khaki trousers, wool Pendleton shirt, and loafers, he leads us to his book-lined office which is separated from the main house by a covered walkway. He sits down at his desk in front of a wall covered with plaques, framed certificates, and old snapshots of friends. Relaxed, he leans back in his swivel chair and lights a cigar. He discusses his work in a rambling, conversational voice.

Despite his informality, he is an imposing figure. His mane of silver hair, the lines which give his face an air of perpetual contemplation, and the things he says, all command respect. But more than any one thing, or series of things, his overall demeanor is that of a man who has, over the course of many years, achieved something of what he set out to do. "I believe in the life chronological, rather than the life existential," one of his characters says. It is obvious that Wallace Stegner believes in the life chronological as well.

RH

Many of your books deal with one aspect or another of the American West. Is this because it's the area you know best, or are there other reasons?

Stegner: There were certainly no other reasons in the beginning. I never set out to become a mouthpiece for the West. In fact, I wasn't that self-conscious about being a Westerner, unless maybe in an embarrassed, culturally inferior sense. My cultural affiliations moved East as I did: from Saskatchewan to Montana to Utah to Wisconsin to Harvard. It never occurred to me I was any spokesman. In fact, look at the books.

Until I came to Stanford in 1945, right at the end of the war, there was essentially no Western bias at all. I had written two Western books and three or four non-Western ones. I think I got the notion there were books to be written about the West sometime *after* I finished one of the most Western of them—the John Wesley Powell biography, BEYOND THE HUNDREDTH MERIDIAN. I had wanted to write that book before I graduated from college because my family had a cabin on the Fish Lake Plateau in Southern Utah. It was country the Powell Survey had gone through, and I had read all the Powell Survey books just to find out about where I lived. I thought they were great. I still do. They're extraordinary books. So, I had the notion Powell was somebody I ought to write about, but I didn't realize how Western a subject he was, and how he would lead me on to a greater self-consciousness about my urban Western-ness.

What finally prompted you to write the book?

Stegner: I suppose it was Benny DeVoto who started me. He asked me to give him some information about Powell so he could use him in THE LITERARY FALLACY as an example of a non-literary person whose work affected all kinds of people more powerfully than a lot of presidents. He used Powell to kick the literary around, and Sinclair Lewis jumped all over him and shot me down too. By that time, I was committed to the Powell book. I learned a lot about the West from right after the Civil War until 1902 because I had to. And that's essentially when the whole West—except for the Gold Rush and the Mormon settlements—happened. After that, many books I wrote somehow wanted to be about the West. I started JOE HILL because I heard that ballad, "I Dreamed I Saw Joe Hill Last Night" and got interested in the songs people had died to. But where it led, of course, was right back West.

In WOLF WILLOW *you speak of "... the inescapable ambivalence of the American conscience experienced by those who lived on the American Frontier." Do you see the West as a microcosm of the American conscience or experience?*

Stegner: Yes, I think so. When I used the word "West," I was thinking of the intermountain West, not the Pacific coast which was settled earlier. The mountains and plains were filled in from both coasts much later. In Saskatchewan I was part of a family which was plowing virgin buffalo grass. We were doing to Saskatchewan what people had done to Kansas in the 1860's. We were literally seventy-five years behind any understanding of our own acts. And I don't think those things change so much. It's easy to dream when you see a lot of open country around you. It may be a may have no validity at all, but it's possible to imagine your way back, to see the time when the first white men saw that country. It's easy to imagine you might lay hands on a piece of that yourself. So, the American Dream, which is a rapacious dream, keeps cropping up. Go to Alaska, and you can watch these very sturdy Alaskan types reproducing exactly the patterns that cut over Michigan and plowed up the buffalo grass. I like these people in a way, but in another way I find them terribly dangerous and terribly unaware that what they most love, their country and their wilderness, is precisely what is most exposed to their kind of destruction. This seems to be an American pattern: we really do destroy what we love. There are many things about the West which make it laggard, backward, but I would say it's a microcosm. It's only a matter of time before the West goes essentially the same way as the rest of the country, if it hasn't gone that way already.

Despite this awareness that we destroy what we love, your books, in relation to many modern novels, seem relatively optimistic in tone.

Stegner: Optimistic?

For example, at the end of THE BIG ROCK CANDY MOUNTAIN, *Bruce says, "It was good to have been along and shared it."* IN ALL THE LITTLE LIVE THINGS *Joe Allston says, "I shall be richer all my life for this sorrow." In general, it seems your novels deal with people who experience great suffering or hardship, yet manage to maintain a tone of affirmation. This seems to us optimistic.*

Stegner: That pleases me to hear. I wasn't really aware of it, but I guess you're right. I was about to say my optimism is past history because I finished THE BIG ROCK CANDY MOUNTAIN in 1941, but I did do it again in ALL THE LITTLE LIVE THINGS, and I'm probably going to do it again in the book I'm writing now. I guess I'm not a very complete cynic, but I wouldn't have dared call myself an optimist. I guess what I would have said is if you can stand life, if you can just *barely* stand it, it's still in your favor. What can Joe Allston do except that? That's a Manichean book: the principle of evil is at least as strong as the principle of good. But I don't understand, quite, people who write books out of hatred or despair. I don't believe their despair, for one thing, because, if it's true despair, you don't write the book. I write about ordinarily decent people, and it seems to me that these very decent people have as much business in a book as Candys or Portnoys. I couldn't write black humor if I wanted to, and I don't really believe in the absurd and the grotesque—unless, as in Faulkner, they're attached to something else, to a very strong, enduring traditionalism. I don't believe someone like Flannery O'Connor who emphasizes the grotesque because she believes you have to shout at a deaf man. That annoys me. I'm not deaf. Not yet, anyway. I don't suppose I've avoided the macabre or the horrible, but it certainly isn't my obsession, and it doesn't fill a lot of pages. A father rubbing his son's nose in his own dung isn't especially nice, or necessarily even realistic. It's an explosion into fury which amounts to the grotesque. But that's almost the only scene in THE BIG ROCK CANDY MOUNTAIN like that. It's my faith that fiction is dramatized belief, and my beliefs include a notion that, if you dislike life, there's an easy way out.

If fiction is belief, what compels one man to write philosophy and another to write fiction?

Stegner: I suppose a knack for dramatization. Philosophy is undramatized belief, analyzed belief. Almost everything you write is belief in one form or other. History is a form of belief. You make it as you write it. It's an artifact you shape in the pattern of your belief, often an unconscious one.

What about Shakespeare? Can you find a single pattern of belief behind Hamlet and Lear and Othello?

Stegner: I see what you're getting at. You don't see the little moustached figure behind that huge variety of characters. But I think I could find a kind of code in Shakespeare. It would take some doing because there's nobody so invisible, except perhaps Faulkner. What Shakespeare had, what Faulkner had, was an extraordinary capacity for identifying with one person after another, a mime's capacity, or a ventriloquist's capacity for being the master of many voices. But underneath, if you hunt long enough, you get—not exactly a code, nothing so rigid as a code—a set of decencies, perhaps. Somehow or other Kent comes off better in your imagination than Regan or Goneril. We judge Shakespeare's people by their acts; and it was in the presentation of their acts that he communicated *his* judgements of them.

Are your characters based on people you know?

Stegner: It's obvious they're based on real people. If they weren't, they would be gargoyles. I wouldn't be capable of making anyone up except as a cartoon. But a character in depth, meant to be in the round, is going to be taken from people I've known, sometimes from two or three combined, but clearly from real people. Obviously, what feeds my imagination is observed reality. It may be observed personally, or from books, or even from historical documents. But then, I'm prejudiced in favor of realistic novels, novels which reflect the experiences of a literal people in a literal society. The writers who reinforce my beliefs strongly—which is one way of responding to books—are Conrad and Chekhov and Turgenev. Lately, I've been catching up on Solzhenitsyn. I don't think there are any contemporary Americans writing novels of the stature of CANCER WARD or THE FIRST CIRCLE, and the fact that I don't think so is probably a sign I'm an anachronism.

You mentioned historical documents. Many of your books make wide use of letters, diaries, songs, medical reports—documents of all kinds. Is there an aesthetic principle involved?

Stegner: Yes, I think so. Again, I don't see any reason to avoid reality. In fact, I see a lot of reasons to make maximum use of it. Drieser used documents in AN AMERICAN TRAGEDY. Truman Capote did pretty much the same in that non-fictional novel of his. It's certainly not a newly-invented form. In MOBY DICK, all those chapters on cetology are partly a change of pace, but also a change

of intention. It's almost as if the real and the surreal are posed side by side. You get some of the same effect if you read HUCKLEBERRY FINN and LIFE ON THE MISSISSIPPI simultaneously. Twain separated the real and the fictional, but Melville combined them, and the combination helped the book by providing contrast. Documents are a way to avoid depending on any single point of view, a way of seeing all around a thing.

You make wide use of documents in ANGLE OF REPOSE.

Stegner: Sure. It's one of the advantages of using Lyman Ward as a narrator. Some of the documents are literally letters from this lady's files. A few of them are almost unchanged, some are half changed, and some are totally changed. Sometimes I'm utilizing documents, and sometimes I'm writing pretend-documentary. All of which, it seems to me, is making maximum use of the tools that are there. It gives you maximum freedom.

What determines the point where the reality ends and the fiction begins?

Stegner: You can't answer that briefly. The lady I used as a model for Susan Ward was taken very much as her letters showed her. But at certain points I wanted her to go over the edge. If she was fastidious, I made her more fastidious. For instance, she won't pick up a handkerchief the old woodcutter throws up to get his pay in. I stretched her to that point. Because she had a little flirtation with a young man in one of the mining camps, I carried that all the way to the fateful infidelity that she took so seriously, that her husband took so seriously. I put her through all kinds of wringers that she never went through in real life. Her real life was perfectly placid, and she lived to be ninety-six. Basing a novel on an individual life, you use only the amount of fiction necessary to make the novel go the way you want. Obviously, you're steering it, or finding out, at least, the way the book wants to go. And if it wants to go toward infidelity, you're going to make some fictional additions to the lady's biography.

Your books lead a life of their own then? You don't plan them before you start writing?

Stegner: Well, if I do, the plan doesn't stick. I used to write elaborate scenarios in the Sinclair Lewis fashion, but the books didn't want to go that way at all. I've begun two or three books without any clear idea of an ending. ALL THE LITTLE LIVE THINGS was one. Sometimes I do know the end, but not how to get there. Now, even if I did know, I don't think I'd write an outline. I wouldn't want to be bound by it because my methods get more and more uneconomic: there's much more trial and error. Things come off the page almost by accident, and I depend on that. If they're right, they stay; if they're not right after a reading or two and a rewriting or two, they'll go out. By the time I've got a first draft, I've written everything fifteen times and read it thirty-five, just trying to learn from my own words where I'm going.

That's a tremendous amount of work for someone who writes long novels, and you seem to prefer long novels. Why?

Stegner: Well, I've written a number of short novels: REMEMBER-ING LAUGHTER, ON A DARKLING PLAIN, FIRE AND ICE, A FIELD GUIDE TO WESTERN BIRDS, GENESIS. All are a hundred to a hundred and fifty pages long, essentially long short stories. I can't seem to do an extended and serious picture of characters within a social context in a short space. I wish sometimes I could. You have to live with people in a book a little time, maybe a long time, before they achieve the reality they ought to have. I found that out early. I was in graduate school, living in Reno one summer, and I had to read a lot of eighteenth-century novels, including CLARISSA HARLOWE. I read a volume a day for eight days and I swear, by the time I was through, I knew Clarissa Harlowe better than I ever knew any-body: alive, dead, fictional, or real. The reason is partly duration. It's living in the same house with that character and reading her letters and following her down the street. Short stories always come to the corner, but never go around it. They take you to the point of change, but don't explore the change or follow it out.

Novels have to go around the corner and follow out the changes. That takes time and that takes pages. If you write the way I do, it takes a lot of pages.

We had the impression that some of your work, particularly ANGLE OF REPOSE, *is intentionally placid at the beginning. The book builds toward the climax, a single act of infidelity, very slowly. Is there something more involved than duration?*

Stegner: E. M. Forster has a habit of doing that. I don't know whether I learned it from him or not. Probably not, because he never really was that much of a favorite of mine. His books proceed quietly for three hundred pages and peak in a great burst, an explosion, at the end of something very quiet. That kind of contrast is an artistic principle it seems foolish to overlook. A book should build like music. That's really all it is. It's compression, and it's space, intensity and opening up, quick passages and slow, loud and soft. You gain by contrast and the anticipation it creates. You gain through a deliberate artistic delay in the slow passages because nobody reading can avoid expecting that sooner or later something's going to happen. You build a very low voltage suspense. And yet this seems more contrived than it is. Often, I don't suppose I deliberately build toward certain climaxes because very often I don't know where the book is going. I change things to build toward a climax without being aware I'm doing it. But before you're through, it's an accident you see coming. You can see it coming on the page. In ANGLE OF REPOSE I wasn't even thinking, I'm sure, about the building toward that one act of infidelity. And, when it came, if you notice, I blurred that infidelity very, very deliberately. It's ambiguous whether anything happened or not. Probably it didn't. In Victorian terms it didn't make any difference. Infidelity is of many kinds. It's of the mind and spirit as well as of the body. I suspect the people in that culture looked upon one as being as bad as the other. One of the things I was trying to do was suggest the full lives of people who lived in an essentially different culture, in a Victorian, gilded-age time. I was attempting to revive the humanity of an age that nowadays gets laughed out of court.

Anyway, I'm surprised you picked the infidelity as the climax. I would have thought it was Lyman Ward's wild hallucination at the end.

That brings up Lyman Ward's function. He's a character as well as a narrator. The book is telling two stories, one modern, one Victorian, almost simultaneously. Could you explain this?

Stegner: There are several reasons for somebody like Lyman Ward. I'd never written much in the first person singular until I did Joe Allston in ALL THE LITTLE LIVE THINGS. I liked what the method lets you do. It seemed particularly suited for ANGLE OF REPOSE, where I was dealing in two layers of time and where I might want to condense years into a paragraph and expand one Fourth of July into two chapters. I could do it much better through somebody's mouth than as an objective recorder of events. I could avoid awkward things like signs carried across the stage saying, "Nine Months Later." So, one of the reasons for Lyman Ward is to get around time. Another reason is to have someone to evaluate, to comment, though I would add that his comments are not always to be believed. On many things, he's accurate; on some things, he's not. He isn't reliable when he deals with his own life. You're supposed to see around him as well as through him. As far as the two simultaneous stories: If I had simply set out to tell the story of Susan Ward and her marriage in the West, I'm afraid it would have looked like a LADIES' HOME JOURNAL novel. I wanted it more complicated than that. I wanted to say something not only about the humanity of Victorian times, but also about the continuity between past and present and the way one feeds the other. And without some figure like Lyman Ward to be a shuttle in that loom, I don't know how I could have managed to weave.

Lyman says, "I believe in the life chronological, rather than the life existential." As a novelist, do you think your concerns are similar to his?

Stegner: Sure, I expect he was speaking for me then. I do believe in a strong continuity, and I resent like anything that in California nobody is ever taught history in the public schools. They don't have history; they have social studies. Students don't get any history at least until high school and perhaps not until college. By that time they've maybe lost the chance to learn from it. Many of them give me the impression they think the world began yesterday. Sociologists do that to me too. They seem to have no historical sense. They see society as a blueprint that can be changed tomorrow. I don't think it can. Reformers have the same problem.

One last question: are there any essential qualities a writer needs? What makes a good writer?

Stegner: When Frost said, "All an artist needs is samples," he was saying it all. That's what you do. You use samples to illustrate those ideas you want to emphasize, and you leave the rest dark. The initial stirrings of a book are very dim and confused. Sometimes, you have a vague notion that there's something in a certain body of material, something remembered, and you can't find a way of hooking onto it. But it's only a matter of finding it. There's never any question whether a book is there, only of making it available to yourself. You have to learn to become flypaper so all dust will stick to you. That's the writer's function.

NOVELS

Remembering Laughter. Boston: Little, Brown, and Company, 1937. (Dell, 1942.)

On A Darkling Plain. New York: Harcourt, Brace & Company, 1940.

Fire and Ice. New York: Duell, Sloan & Pearce, 1941.

The Big Rock Candy Mountain. New York: Duell, Sloan & Pearce, 1943. (Hill and Wang, 1957.) Published in hardback by Doubleday & Company, 1973.

Second Growth. Boston: Houghton Mifflin, 1947. (Popular Library, 1969.)

The Preacher and the Slave. Boston: Houghton Mifflin, 1950. Reissued as JOE HILL. Garden City: Doubleday & Company, 1969; (Ballantine Books—A Comstock Edition, 1972.)

A Shooting Star. New York: The Viking Press, 1961. (Dell, 1962.)

All the Little Live Things. New York: The Viking Press, 1967. (New American Library, 1968.)

Angle of Repose. Garden City: Doubleday & Company, 1971. (Fawcett Crest, 1972.)

The Spectator Bird. Garden City: Doubleday & Company, 1976.

SHORT STORIES

The Potter's House. Muscatine, Iowa: Prarie Press, 1938.

The Women on the Wall. Boston: Houghton Mifflin, 1950. (Compass Books, 1962.)

The City of the Living. Boston: Houghton Mifflin, 1956.

NON-FICTION

Mormon Country. New York: Duell, Sloan & Pearce, 1942. (Bonanza Books, 1970.)

One Nation. Boston: Houghton Mifflin, 1945. [With the editors of LOOK Magazine.]

Beyond the Hundredth Meridian. Boston: Houghton Mifflin, 1954. (Sentry Editions, 1962.) [About John Wesley Powell and the reopening of the West.]

Wolf Willow. New York: The Viking Press, 1962. (Viking Compass, 1966.)

The Gathering of Zion. New York: McGraw-Hill, 1964. (McGraw-Hill, 1966.)

The Sound of Mountain Water. Garden City: Doubleday & Company, 1969. (Bonanza Books, 1972.)

The Uneasy Chair. Garden City: Doubleday & Company, 1974. [Biography of Bernard DeVoto.]

The Letters of Bernard DeVoto. Garden City: Doubleday & Company, 1975. [Arranged and introduced by Wallace Stegner.]

Jessamyn West

Jessamyn West lives with her husband outside Napa in a two-story wood house with a stone porch in front and a stone patio in the rear. There are trees everywhere. She greets us wearing a dark sweater, slacks, a beaded Indian necklace, and a broad smile.

It is difficult to believe she is the same woman who describes herself as a loner in the autobiographical HIDE AND SEEK. She seems to have no nervousness, hesitancy, or suspicion to overcome. She sits in a rocking chair in front of the fireplace in the living room, a long bookcase covering the wall behind her, and talks about her work—and anything else that comes to mind—with openness and enthusiasm.

During the course of the afternoon, she also provides "beer and wine of all kinds," a curry lunch, and guided sidetrips around the house and grounds. She shows us the bedroom where she works and the small bed-desk she places astride her legs when writing; the bathroom that seems a part of the garden beneath the trees because the wall behind the tub is not a wall at all, but a window; the attic hideaway filled with books; the horse, corral, and barn; and her home away from home, a Dodge Motor Van parked beside the carport. When we comment on her obvious relish for life and her brisk, almost ingenuous vitality, she says, "I had tuberculosis for fifteen years. I have a lot to make up for."

RH

Are writers different from other people?

West: They are probably more experienced in giving themselves away. This accounts, no doubt, for two of their qualities: their obnoxiousness and the stimulation of their talk.

How did you get started as a writer?

West: I remember I was mad about words and reading and writing, but I was brought up in Yorba Linda, California. No one there had ever seen a living writer, and I supposed if you were a writer, you would look in the mirror and see some sign. I remember writing "J. West" lightly with a pencil in a library book. Somehow, that gave me the satisfaction of feeling that if I were not a writer, at least I wrote in a book.

One day, before I had tuberculosis, I started writing something in my journal—I've kept journals all my life, stacks of them—and it was about no one I knew. I wrote for three or four pages, and these people talked, and I knew I had written.

Yet, your first book wasn't published until after your tuberculosis attack, years later. Is there a reason?

West: I had been afraid to write. I thought it was pretentious, lazy, and also that I probably *couldn't* write. I just didn't have the guts. Maybe Quakerdom had something to do with it, or maybe my particular Quakers, the Milhouses. The Milhouses weren't people who took big chances. They did what they could do and thought they could succeed in doing. I heard my grandfather say, "Don't stick your neck out, don't give your self away, don't risk making a fool of yourself." Every writer not only takes a chance of making a fool of himself, he may discover that he actually is a fool. All of these things added together.

What made you start writing seriously then? Was your tuberculosis a stimulus?

West: No, I don't think, as people sometimes say, that tubercular people are ignited by fever into imaginative creation. I would say that, in a way, it would have been impossible for me to write unless I was unable to do anything else. I backed myself into a corner with that sickness. I didn't know how to justify trying to write without every other thing being cut off. Tuberculosis made it possible.

I was at the University of California at Berkeley working for a Ph.D. in English, and the date had been set for my orals when I had a lung hemorrhage. Within three days I was in a sanitorium with far advanced tuberculosis. After two years they sent me home to die with my loved ones. A woman said to me one day, "Jessamyn, why don't you piece a quilt so you could have something to leave for your mother to remember you by." I thought, "What the hell, if it's come to that." I had reached the point when nobody thought it pretentious to write. They thought it was brave, courageous, for this young woman to scribble away as she lay there dying.

I began to write lying in bed at home—I still write in bed—and my husband said, "I'll have these stories printed for you." That drove me crazy. I said, "Look, you're a teacher. If I were a millionairess, and you couldn't get a job, and I said to you, 'I can hire children for you to teach,' would you like that?" He said he wouldn't like that, but he kept nagging me to do something about the stories cluttering up the place. Finally, I said, "I will write twelve stories and send each one to twelve different magazines.

They will all be turned down. Then, do I have your solemn promise that you will let me write away?" He said, "Fine."

Somebody took one, and they began to be taken—not always at first—one by one. Then, Harcourt, Brace wrote me saying they would like to publish a collection of my Quaker stories. I thought they were daft. I thought, "Who in God's name wants to read a whole book of Quaker stories? Would I go into a bookstore and say, 'Do you have any good fiction about Seventh Day Adventists?'"

You couldn't have remembered too much about Indiana since you left there when you were six years old. Why did you choose it as a setting for THE FRIENDLY PERSUASION?

West: It is more difficult for me to write about what is right around me than about what I have to imagine. Roth wrote THE BREAST. Would you ask him how he could do this since he had never been a breast?

Adams wrote WATERSHIP DOWN. Would you ask him how he could do this since he admitted his rabbit knowledge came from a book about rabbits?

Gardner wrote GRENDEL. Would you ask him how he could do this since his acquaintance with fens and mythical monsters was skimpy?

Vonnegut regularly gets planetary beings into his novels. How can he do this having never visited a planet other than our own?

And those hobbits!

The real answer to your question probably is that Indiana is my rabbit, my hobbit, my breast, my planet, my fen-loving monster. I write about it because knowing little about it, I can create it. I am a bigger risk-taker than these others. The Hoosiers can contradict me. No rabbit, hobbit, or breast has been known to speak up in reply to their exploiters.

I admit Indiana isn't very chic. Kids like planets and breasts and rabbits more. But one uses what one has. Indiana was *terra incognita*, and my imagination about it had been stirred by my mother's memories and the words she used to convey those memories.

At the time they sent me home to die, I couldn't bear to think of the life I had had as a young married woman and a student. I'd lost that. I had no future, so my mother gave me Indiana and her life there. Maybe I just don't see the reality in front of my eyes very well, so I create an imagined reality in writing.

Do your mother and father and others you've known appear in your work? Are your characters modeled after real people?

West: Being of my generation and of my temperament, it was hard for me to write frankly about my own people. In THE WITCH DIGGERS Lib Conboy had some of my mother's characteristics, yes, and I think Link Conboy had some of my father's. Bass, in LEAFY RIVERS, had some of my grandfather's characteristics. On the other hand, THE FRIENDLY PERSUASION is one hundred thousand percent fiction. You two could sit here all day, and I couldn't put you in a story. It may be that I'm just not a good conscious observer of human beings; but I think I do do it unconsciously.

Graham Greene feels much the same as I. He says writers should forget their own lives. The bits and pieces you remember should fall down into your unconscious and become compost. When you need something, it's there in the compost heap. You've forgotten it's what you lived through. So, for me, the thing to do in writing is to ask myself questions, not tell myself answers: to ask, What did this man do? What did he feel? and let the answer boil up to the surface.

When the answers boil to the surface how do you decide which answers to include or not?

West: When you make a story, you make a thing. It's like making an urn or a stone wall. You put in what that artifact needs at that point and maybe you leave out things it needs even more.

Do you plot your books in advance at all, then? Do you know how a book is going to end?

West: Malraux wrote a novel which disappeared during the German occupation of Paris. After Paris was liberated, an interviewer said, "You will, of course, rewrite it." Malraux replied, "Certainly not." Asked why, he said, "Because I know the ending." Non-writers don't understand this. Writing is exciting. I feel the same excitement a reader feels because my characters say and do things I don't know they are going to say and do.

I don't think I could start something unless I had an idea where it was going—I couldn't start a short story without the title, and the title usually has something to do with where the story is going—but I may discover as I know more about the people, as they move and express themselves, as they act and interact, that the ending I thought about is not plausible. They would not have done that. Perhaps, I could be a better writer if I outlined. But basically, thinking, plotting, planning is not the way I write. I have sometimes felt that if I wrote a sentence, then tied to the last word of that sentence another word, I'd presently have a book. For the most part, writing is life making itself known to me through words.

Most, though not all, of your characters are basically good. They have their share of human weakness, but they're not evil. Do you think of your work as a whole as being philosophically positive?

West: I have Quaker relatives who believe if you have any aptitude in the use of words, you should be preaching, and I have read writers who had a purpose in writing, who did not want to write a thing that would not somehow elevate, make better, make happier the people who read it.

I am a storyteller, and I do not have that desire to preach. I haven't any formal philosophy. I write because I want someone to feel and experience what I feel and experience, to see what I have seen.

Evil exists, and a writer should be able to depict it, but I have not encountered much evil in my life. This is a handicap for a writer, an enormous handicap. If for three hundred years all of your people have been Quakers, and if you lie in bed for fifteen years with people taking care of you, you don't have a great deal of experience with evil.

Once, I started to write a story about a guy people would hate. As I wrote the story, I became that man, and all the hate went out of me. I couldn't hate myself, and I couldn't make my reader feel what I didn't feel. Maybe this is an indication of my deficiencies as a writer. I don't know how to slant a story. The craftsman—the hack even—knows how to make the reader feel the emotions appropriate to the fictive situation.

All of my tears on a page or my mounting blood pressure mean nothing to the reader. I may feel that I am Tess, hanged, or Hester with her A, but what counts in writing is the ability to make the reader identify himself with the character. Perhaps the combination of the two—tears in the heart and craft in the hand—makes the master. Dickens had both. It is my ambition someday to write about a truly evil man. It probably won't come off.

Earlier, you mentioned you still wrote in bed. Is there any particular reason? Could you discuss some of your other working habits?

West: It just seems like the place to write. It would seem businesslike to write at a desk. And, if you're a housewife, there are two good reasons for staying in bed. One, you have on your nightgown or pajamas and can't go running to the door at the knock of strangers. Also, once you're up and dressed, you see ten thousand things that need doing. So, I wake up and get some coffee or orange juice and go back to bed. I write everything in longhand. I could type at one time, and I suppose I still could, but it's not very easy to have a typewriter on your stomach in bed.

How do you revise?

West: I revise day by day and page by page until it seems I can't make it any better. Then, I let that stand and go on. After it's finished, I send it to my typist. It looks quite different when it comes home, and I usually change that, and it's typed a second time.

You leave it alone then?

West: Yes. Sometimes I have thought that I should put everything away for a year, but I can't stand to reread it unless it is still molten. Even if I were to reread a published book of mine now and see something I didn't like, I wouldn't want to be mixed up with it again. I've already given birth to that baby.

You've written short stories, novels, an autobiography, a play, and edited an anthology. Is there one form you prefer?

West: I certainly did, at first, prefer short stories. I expect I'm a novelist now. It may be that is somewhat a matter of age. When you're younger, a short story is a form that more quickly conveys emotion. It takes less staying power and more feeling.

Are you working on anything now?

West: I have a new book coming out called THE MASSACRE AT FALL CREEK which has been taken by The Literary Guild and The Reader's Digest book clubs. The publication had to be postponed because the book clubs had just published Michener's CENTENNIAL which has a massacre in it. They didn't think the public was ready to have one massacre after another rammed down its throat. I had the manuscript finished last fall. I've just finished another book called THE WOMAN SAID YES.

Would you mind talking about them?

West: THE MASSACRE AT FALL CREEK is about the first time white men in the United States were ever tried and then hanged for the killing of Indians. This happened in Indiana. THE WOMAN SAID YES is non-fiction. It's about my mother and myself and my sister, something on the order of HIDE AND SEEK, but more about them than me.

Is THE MASSACRE AT FALL CREEK a history?

West: No. I don't want to write history. That's reporting. I'm not a reporter. Almost nothing is known about the incident. Ten or twelve pages written twenty-five years later by one of the prosecuting attorneys and two pages written by the man who was the Indian agent are all that remain. The courthouse with all the records burned down. Everything in the book except the historical incident is fiction.

Why did you choose this particular incident for a book?

West: I've read a lot about Indiana. I had read about this incident and thought a lot about those murdered Indians. Also, I have Indian blood: my grandmother was half Indian. I don't know whether that had anything to do with it or not. Anyway, the subject was vivid—and significant.

Are there any writers you particularly admire?

West: One day I was downcast when one of Harcourt, Brace's editors was here. I said to Margaret, "Why can't I write like Eudora Welty?" She said, "Look, you don't have Eudora Welty's pen. You have Jessamyn West's pen. It's a different pen. Use it as best you can. That's all you can do. There are some people who like you better than Eudora Welty."

Sure, I would have liked to have been a Eudora Welty or a Carson McCullers or a Flannery O'Connor—I don't know whether I would want to be a Joyce Carol Oates or not—but I think what this gal told me is the truth. More or less you do what you can with what you've got.

I do have a great reverence for Hemingway. He changed our use of the English language. In his economy, his choice of detail, his use of simple strong words and sentences, he was able to make a short story convey the reality of fiction with the emotion of poetry.

I read everybody, almost. I remember being in Paris in 1928 for a month or so, just at the time I believe Hemingway and Stein and the Fitzgeralds were in and out of that city. I never saw them, but I did at once discover Shakespeare & Co. and bought one of the blue paper-backed copies of ULYSSES they were publishing. It was against the law to bring a copy into the United States. I was traveling with a trunk, of course. It was half-filled on my return with stone jars of English marmalade. The sight of a jam-crazy tourist so repelled the inspector of imports that he never got beneath the jam to the Joyce. The jam is gone, but Joyce remains.

NOVELS

The Friendly Persuasion. New York: Harcourt, Brace & Company, 1945. (Harcourt, Brace & World, 1966; Avon Books, 1970.)

The Witch Diggers. New York: Harcourt, Brace & Company, 1951. (Bantam Books, 1952, 1964; Avon Books, 1970.)

Cress Delahanty. New York: Harcourt, Brace & World, 1953. (Pocket Books, 1955; Avon Books, 1970.)

*Little Men. Ballantine Books, 1954. (Reissued as **The Chilekings**, Ballantine Books, 1967.)

South of the Angels. New York: Harcourt, Brace & World, 1960. (Fawcett Crest, 1961; Avon Books, 1972.)

A Matter of Time. New York: Harcourt, Brace & World, 1966. (Avon Books, 1970.)

Leafy Rivers. New York: Harcourt, Brace & World, 1967. (Avon Books, 1970.)

Except for Me and Thee. New York: Harcourt, Brace & World, 1967. (Avon Books, 1970.)

The Massacre at Fall Creek. New York: Harcourt Brace Jovanovich, 1975. (Fawcett, 1976.)

SHORT STORIES

Love, Death, and the Ladies' Drill Team. New York: Harcourt, Brace & World, 1955. (Harbrace, 1968.)

Crimson Ramblers of the World, Farewell. New York: Harcourt Brace Jovanovich, 1970.

NON-FICTION

The Reading Public. New York: Harcourt, Brace & Company, 1952.

Love is Not What You Think. New York: Harcourt, Brace & World, 1960.

POETRY

The Secret Look. New York: Harcourt Brace Jovanovich, 1974.

*Published in paperback only.

AUTOBIOGRAPHY

To See the Dream. New York: Harcourt, Brace & World, 1957. (Avon Books, 1974.)

Hide and Seek. New York: Harcourt Brace Jovanovich, 1973.

The Woman Said Yes. New York: Harcourt Brace Jovanovich, 1976.

OTHER

A Mirror For the Sky. New York: Harcourt, Brace & Company, 1948. [An opera based on the life of Audubon; original conception by Raoul Pere du Bois.]

The Quaker Reader. Now York: The Viking Press, 1962. (Viking Compass, 1969.) [Selected and introduced by Jessamyn West.]

Index